GREAT CREDIT NOW

SET YOUR GPS FOR POSITIVE SUCCESS

TIPS, TOOLS, AND TALES OF MANAGING THE GAME OF CREDIT SUCCESSFULLY

AUTHENTIC ENDEAVORS PUBLISHING
CLARKS SUMMIT, PA

Copyright © 2016 Great Credit Now

All rights reserved. No part of this publication may be reproduced, distributed or transmitted in any form or by any means, including photocopying, recording, or other electronic or mechanical methods, without the prior written permission of the publisher, except in the case of brief quotations embodied in critical reviews and certain other noncommercial uses permitted by copyright law. For permission requests, write to the publisher, addressed "Attention: Permissions Coordinator," at the address below.

Authentic Endeavors Publishing
P.O. Box 704
Clarks Summit, PA 18411
www.authenticdedavorspublishing.com

Cover and Interior Design: Ambicionz
www.ambicionz.com

Disclaimer: This book is a compilation of stories from numerous experts who have each contributed a chapter. As such, the views expressed in each chapter are of those who submitted their stories.

Great Credit Now —1st ed.
ISBN 978-0-9982105-0-6

CONTENTS

FOREWORD

Credit and debt are two of the most asked about topics when it comes to understanding finances. Credit can either be a tool in building wealth and success or, without proper management, cause financial ruin. Everywhere you look today there is an advertisement for a new credit card. It's so easy to buy things and take vacations using those credit cards...it's called instant gratification. But, do you have the money in the bank to pay for what you are buying on credit? Or are you digging yourself into a financial hole that will need a long ladder for you to get out of before it caves in on you? I happen to love my credit cards and use them often but...I also make sure I pay them off at the end of each month.

As a national spokesperson on the topic of financial education and a member of the first President's Advisory Council on Financial Literacy, I'm here to urge you to use credit wisely. Building financial strength and creating wealth is a process that may or may not include the use of credit, depending on your individual circumstances. Consumer debt, if misused, is one of the ways that individuals can falter financially.

Create a financial game plan that will make the use of credit a positive experience for you. My suggestion is to use whatever tools are available to you that will support you in keeping your experience with credit a positive one.

You can become a master of credit…or a slave to credit! There is very little in between. The choice is yours.

The authors of the stories in this book share quite candidly how credit has affected their lives, and some of them share how they were able to shift their experiences from negative to positive.

As a financial educator, I invite you to explore the stories with the intention of learning…from other's mistakes and from other's successes. Learn how credit can be an asset to creating wealth and how consumer debt can easily trap you or be used for your financial benefit.

It is my mission to inspire change for individuals and businesses throughout the globe. My expertise and passion for financial literacy has inspired me to create programs that teach the management of finances and wealth creation.

As the founder and CEO of Pay Your Family First, I have developed award winning tools that are currently utilized by individuals, parents and educators to inspire positive financial stewardship and the entrepreneurial spirit.

My hope is that the information you glean from these stories will lead you to a brighter financial future and a powerfully positive experience with the use of credit in your life.

To your financial success!

Sharon Lechter CPA CGMA
CEO of Pay Your Family First
Author of *Think and Grow Rich for Women*, Co-author of *Outwitting the Devil, Three Feet From Gold, Rich Dad Poor Dad* and 14 other books in the Rich Dad series.

CHAPTER 1

YOUR CREDIT JOURNEY

Rusty Breese

Understanding credit data and the importance it plays in today's society isn't as convoluted as the credit experts make it seem. Consumers spend many unwanted hours and dollars researching every angle they can to chase the almighty 850 credit score.

How does obsession and necessity differ or compare during this impeded journey? One must look deep inside to see if this is a forced journey or a planned expedition. Either way the road will be bumpy at times, exciting and adventurous but mostly it will be rewarding.

Behavioral tendencies contribute a fair amount to how successful you will be credit score wise or worthy to a lender's underwriting guidelines. We live in a competitive environment and the mysterious three-digit score attached to your credit data measures your ability to repay a loan compared to others striving to obtain a similar loan. Sure you may be offered the consolation prize (a higher rate) for having a lower score, but chances are the prize given helps the grantor more than the recipient.

Like any uncertain excursion the first thing you need is a map, in this case the map will be a copy of your credit report. Your report can be obtained by any of the three major credit providers, Equifax, TransUnion, or Experian. This map will offer and pressure many detours. When you come to the forks in the road, it will be best to already know the road signs.

To interpret the signs better, it will help you to know that the credit reporting agencies host over a billion credit accounts daily. Your credit data, along with over 250 million other reports, rely exclusively on the accounts being reported correctly to each credit bureau. One might think with today's technology this would be a simple task, but unfortunately there are way too many variables for this to happen. Common mistakes found on a credit report come straight from the creditor you currently do business with or the ones from the past. Employees from these companies are responsible to make sure your account is being reported correctly and timely to the credit bureaus. Once it has been reported, it becomes your responsibility to check the accuracies and authenticities. I guess it would help if you knew what to look for, so I will become your tour guide.

In order to understand your credit data, you will have to look over the entire report. It will help if you locate the oldest accounts being reported. Circle the open date on both the open and closed accounts. The overall aged account plays a significant role. Be sure to keep the oldest revolving credit account open and up to date. For you first time travelers, a revolving credit account will be a credit card. The other accounts, mortgage loans, auto loans, bank, finance, and student loans will be categorized as an installment loan.

Credit scoring algorithms, although complex, can be very simple. Key factors are going to be the age, combined age, credit limits, balances, usage, variety, and payment history. The weight is distributed among the factors with the balance to high credit ratio along with the age of the account being at the top. Discipline will come into play when you are at the fork in the road and you want to make a purchase with a credit card. Do you go to the left and charge the item without regard to a higher percentage balance to high credit ratio on a most recently obtained card or do you make the purchase on an older charge card? Do you go to the right, charge only the amount you are prepared to pay off before the creditor reports to the credit bureau? You may be thinking, doesn't the creditor report to the credit bureau each time I pay on the account? The answer is no they don't, also it's important to know the report date and due date are entirely different. Both are important. If you pay after the due date your credit score will drop considerably, and if you pay before the report date your score will likely stay the same or increase. So, it would be wise to know from your creditor when they report to the credit bureaus, whether you are able to pay the balance in full or not.

A major bump in the road is the misconception of when high credit usage instead of credit limit being reported has the same impact on the credit score. A credit limit is the maximum approved amount you can spend while the high credit is the maximum amount you have used from your approved credit limit. When a credit card grantor approves your request for an account, a credit line or credit limit is established. Unfortunately, the credit limit is not always the number being reported to the credit bureaus, the maximum amount you have charged reports. This is a common mistake, which will affect the score in a detrimental way. Commonly, the high credit or usage is reported instead or, even less good, it will show zero. Since credit scoring is based on the balance to credit limit algorithms you can imagine what happens to your score if one or several accounts fall into this category. I will give you an example: your credit limit on revolving credit card A is $5,000 but you have only charged $2,000 and you have a $500 outstanding balance. You will be scored based on the $2,000 being reported which will lower your score. Point Deduction Technology software will determine how many points you may actually lose from the reporting errors.

WHAT IS POINT DEDUCTION TECHNOLOGY?

Point Deduction Technology® is Scientific Analytical Mathematical Software, based on rigorous credit weight algorithms, which analyzes credit data to identify where the impacts are placed on a credit file. The software analyzes an electronic version of a credit report and assigns a point deduction number per item, both positive and negative. The numbers assigned range from 0 to 100+ depending on the type of accounts being reported. The software also determines where most errors occur on a credit report and how many points may be recovered by having the credit data corrected. This Technology will serve as your compass. You will be able to move forward towards your goals and if you get lost along the way, you will be able to get back on track.

Whether this is your first trip or if you have traveled already, your first step will be to obtain a copy of your credit report. Identity theft is rapidly growing worldwide so it's important to know what may be reported. Will checking your own credit lower your score? The reporting agencies distinguish between soft and hard pulls. When your credit is checked before issuing its line of credit it's called a hard pull and it counts against your score. Personal requests fall under soft pulls, which do not reflect negatively on the evaluation.

ESTABLISHING CREDIT FOR THE FIRST TIME CAN BECOME OVERWHELMING SINCE THERE WILL BE MANY OPPORTUNITY OFFERS IN FRONT OF YOU.

My suggestion is you research secured credit card offers. A secured credit card means you will be asked to open a savings account with a major lender who will then match your credit line with your deposit. Although your deposit secures the credit line banks are still at risk so it's important you keep balances low if you are unable to pay it off each month. You will make payments and by doing it on time, will create a credit score. If possible you should open multiple (two or three) secured credit accounts. Your deposited money is held safely in the bank and will be returned to you in the future once your card balance is zeroed and the account is closed. Secured credit cards also help you if you have had some past bumps in the road. It is the best way to re-establish credit.

While building a successful credit profile, you must follow the rules of the road. It would be helpful if you can charge and pay your account in full each time before the report date monthly. You must make sure the minimum payment is made by the due date each month. Don't apply for a bunch of new credit right away. Test drive the credit you have recently established to make sure you stay on the right road. Your experience will help grow your credit score and in time other credit offers will become available.

For those who have already established older accounts, control your speed, (balances) and don't be so quick to close revolving credit card accounts. Open accounts spell available, potential debt, so better to close them, runs the legend. But experts agree that most creditors want to see at least two or three pieces of active credit to prove you can manage debt responsibly. Remember, everything reported to the credit bureau other than public record information has a point value but not everything has a point deduction.

WHAT IS REVOLVING CREDIT?

Credit Cards issued and used by consumers such as bank cards, departments store, and gas cards are categorized as Revolving Credit. Your Revolving Credit does not require a set number of payments and you may use or borrow up to your preset credit limit. Since your available credit decreases and increases as funds are borrowed and then repaid, the credit scoring algorithms will insure higher scores if used properly.

WHAT IS INSTALLMENT CREDIT?

Installment is a type of credit that has a fixed number of payments, in contrast to revolving credit. Granted credit lines are conditionally set up based on fixed monthly payments at regular intervals. Installment loans are designed for big purchases such as housing, automobiles, furniture and personal loans. Nearly all installment loans will be collateralized by items you intend to finance, with the exception of student loans. Your payment history will be reported to the credit bureaus so it's important all scheduled payments are made before the due date each month. If you default on a payment, all previous payments will be forfeited and the lender may take possession of the items you financed. Scoring algorithms suggest future automobile and home loans in your credit profile to maximize your credit score.

HOW DOES MY CREDIT DATA EFFECT MY CREDIT SCORE?

Payment history tops the list so making your payments on time is critical. Most of the over 50 scoring algorithms list payment history at a 35 percent factor in the make up of your score. Occasionally the payments made will not always reflect the true payment history on your credit report. Check the date of last activity and months reviewed to verify the last time your payment was recorded. Also check to make sure any unwanted late payments haven't been reported. Making a payment late will quickly lower your credit score and only time will completely recover all the lost points.

THIRTY PERCENT OF YOUR CREDIT SCORE CONSISTS OF CREDIT UTILIZATION.

Let me explain the importance again on why you must make sure your true credit limit and balances are being reported correctly. Payment history and credit utilization make up 65 percent of your score, yet studies show this is where most common errors occur. Focus on this road even when it gets bumpy at times to allow enough time to correct the mistakes. On a side note, be sure to continue utilizing your revolving credit, rather than closing an older account, make a small charge and pay it off immediately. Going longer than six months without utilization may drop your score.

HOW LONG YOU HAVE HAD ESTABLISHED ACCOUNTS IS ALSO IMPORTANT.

Too many times an older revolving account is forgotten about and a creditor may actually close the account. Important factors expressed here is you will be based on the length of time each account has been opened separately and combined overall. You will also be scored on the most recent action taken. Be sure to check the open date on every open account to verify its accuracy. All accounts will read just the average length so be careful when opening up too many new accounts. Long term positive financial behavior results in a higher credit score.

NEW CREDIT AND A COMBINATION OF DIFFERENT TYPE ACCOUNTS CONTRIBUTE TO YOUR CREDIT SCORE.

Combining a good blend of revolving credit and installment loans offers lenders less risk predictability during the repayment process. One would figure having a good credit score with established long term accounts with no reported late payments or other derogatory accounts and low balances compared to credit limits is all you need, right? Unfortunately, the errors and omissions in credit reporting become an integral part of the equation.

Your destination has been mapped out, the detours and roadblocks accounted for, warning and speed signs identified, gauges checked, compass and tools available, a how to guide for emergencies, the right amount of fuel, and the time it will take to start the journey.

One important step is how to finance this voyage. I would suggest setting up a rigorous budget to assure a vacation like atmosphere versus a long walk because you are broken down on the side of the road hungry and not sure where you are. Check your map and look for the toll roads you will be on so you will stay prepared. The money you invest into establishing and maintaining a healthy credit profile will ultimately save you thousands in higher interest rates.

Follow the information provided and with the right patience, courage and confidence you will accomplish your credit and financial goals. Don't focus on the credit scores, only the credit data, remember if the data is right your score will keep becoming maximized. See you on the road.

ABOUT THE AUTHOR

Rusty M Bresse CEO of Cred-Logix Inc, holds a Bachelor of Arts Degree in Business and has helped trail blaze the credit industry since 1981.

Understanding the need for credit and financial literacy Mr. Bresse began to develop innovative products for the home and auto buying industry. Spearheading the first online access credit and financial wellness company, Mr. Bresse has worked directly with consumers and businesses educating them on credit laws, credit bureau strategies, credit investigations, credit behavior, and how credit scoring would play a significant role in our lives.

Mr. Bresse created Point Deduction Technology® a Scientific Analytical Mathematical Software, based on rigorous credit weight algorithms used to analyze credit data and identify where the impacts are placed on a credit file. Mr. Bresse continues to develop credit and financial analytic software used by loan originators and consumers Internationally. Mr. Bresse is married and the father to 6 children.

Learn about the credit management tool at www.scorenavigator.com

CHAPTER 2

ACHIEVING SUCCESS INSPIRATION THAT GAVE ME THE COURAGE TO BE A FINANCIAL THINK TANK

Anne Brille

October 16, 1983. My life as I knew it, at the young age of twelve would change forever. I remember it clearly. We were living in our new house; my parents, my ten-year-old sister and me. Being a young family, Dad 37, Mom 30; everyone was happy, healthy and looking forward to all that was ahead. On that day, the one I will never forget, we got a phone call from the hospital; my dad had an accident. We rushed to the hospital and a few hours later the doctor told us that my father passed away. How could this have happened? A soccer ball? Life as I knew it literally stopped in that moment. My very healthy 37-year-old Dad passed away because someone kicked a soccer ball into my dad's chest and his heart stopped. That soccer game accident took my father away from our family forever. My Dad was an amazing man. He loved me and my sister. I remember him being an amazing husband and awesome father; I loved him so much and even though he was only with me until the age of 12 he taught me so much. A big part of who I am today is because of him.

We had moved to our house July 31 of that same year, 1983, and sadly, there was no life insurance policy on my Dad when he died. My mom was a very strong and hard working woman who worked in the fur Industry. After Dad died, she would leave the house at 7 o'clock every morning to go to downtown Toronto. It was a one hour bus and subway ride to where she worked until 4 o'clock every day. When she arrived home at 5 o'clock we would all have dinner together, then she would begin working her second job at 6 o'clock sewing fur skins until 2 o'clock in the morning. She did this five days a week.

Being the older daughter, I took charge of some responsibility. My mom relied on me to go to the bank to deposit her checks since her job did not provide direct deposit. She would get paid on Thursday, and I would go to the bank every Friday to make sure the money would be there so the mortgage payment would come out of her account on time and all the bills were paid. I was always scared that the home would be taken away from us if I didn't make the bill payments on time. I even had nightmares about it. I took my responsibilities very seriously. This process of making sure the money was in the bank so that things could be paid on time so early on in life, taught me the importance of properly managing money. That was instilled in me at the age of 12. Sometimes life hands us something that causes us to grow up really fast.

Every day after school when my sister and I got home, I would clean the house and cook dinner. I would actually cook a full meal every night then we would wait by the door for my mom to come home at 5 o'clock. Sometimes when the weather was rough and the buses would be a little delayed, my sister and I would wait at the door for her to come home. We didn't have cell phones then, so there was no way for mom to phone while she was on the subway or bus to let us know she would be late because of a delay, so we would just wait. As soon as Mom came home our world became better and brighter; we both love her dearly and she knows that we know she loves us. Everything she did and still does today is for me and my sister. From that early age on, through having taken on the responsibility of handling money, I learned the importance of money, timing and being held responsible for what you owe.

After about two years of solid work, Mom met an amazing man, got remarried and we became a new family. The transition to the new blended family with a new stepdad and a new stepbrother was not easy at first but today I'm very happy to say that I have an awesome relationship with both my stepfather and my stepbrother.

After high school, I got accepted to the University of Toronto and that same summer I started working at a bank. A friend of my mother's had been working in a different department there and knew I was looking for a job, so I applied. I was actually hired on my nineteenth birthday to cover hours while other employees were on vacation and a month later I was offered a permanent part time job. It worked with the schedule I would soon have at the university, so I stayed on while I was attending college.

A few ladies within the bank had taken me under their wing and really taught me the importance of making payments on time and putting money aside for investments to start building for my future, even at the age of 19. Personally, I was more interested in finding the right clothes, wearing the best make up and going out and having fun. I listened to their advice though and I saved anyway. Then I made sure my sister also learned what I was being reinforced in me; bills must be paid on time and money must be put aside for her future. No matter how small the amount is, always put aside something for the future. I did that faithfully with every paycheck, using savings bonds and a retirement account as a way to save.

During this time, I was also learning the importance of and how to manage my own credit card. I was taught that when I used the card to make a purchase, I should have the money to pay it in full when the bill came. So every month, I made sure that the credit card was paid in full. Already knowing the importance of paying on time, I was now learning the importance of building a solid credit score for myself.

After six years in banking and after university it was time to look for a permanent full time job. Most places that I applied saw me as being too young for a more senior role, but I was independent and smart. I took a job as an administrative assistant for a senior financial planner at his company. I wasn't a very good administrator, so I used what I had learned to create a business plan, and then convinced the owners to send me to Scottsdale, Arizona where I would work with a telemarketing expert. My plan was to start up a telemarketing company for them.

They thought it was a good idea, so they funded the cost of the course, airfare and all the expenses for the week that I was there.

So at about the age of 25, I started a telemarketing division for that company which paid me a percentage of the commission on all the deals that were set up by the telemarketers for the agents who were looking for new clients. After about two years, I was hired as a senior Financial Advisor for a financial planning company that gave me a portfolio to grow. With the help of the schooling that was mandatory for the position and gave me some industry designations, I was able to grow that portfolio by 155%! I did really well, and at the age of 29, I made $112,000.

With money that I had been saving and the good credit score I had developed through the discipline of paying on time and always staying at less than 50% of my credit limit when I did spend using credit, I was able to buy my house that year. Because it was instilled in me to handle money wisely, I and my then boyfriend, who is now my husband were able to put down 25% to purchase our dream home. We still live in that home we bought together and are a very happy family with our little girl and our puppy.

I'm an entrepreneur. I'm running my own business and I consider myself successful in my own definition of what success means. I'm able to do things for my mother, for my little girl and for my family that I never thought I'd be able to do. Working smart and well does pay off. The importance of building net worth along with building your credit that I learned at such a very young age has brought me wealth. I'm happy to say that right now at 43 years old I consider myself to be a successful business owner and entrepreneur, mother, daughter, wife, aunt, godmother, sister and friend.

I now teach others how to get ahead in life and support their credit. I teach about how important it is in Canada to have that credit knowledge as part your life in order to get a mortgage. I teach my clients what I learned from a variety of training, the advice of others and from what was successful for me. It's so important to keep credit balances at less than 50% of the card's limit and to pay on time each month. Your score will build when you keep the balance low. Be sure to pay all of your bills on time and save something every paycheck. You are building your future. When it comes time to get a mortgage to buy a house, you'll be in good shape to get a good interest rate.

Remember... nothing changes until something changes. If you want to see the change in your financial future, you must make those changes today. If you are struggling to figure out a plan that works, please feel free to consult with me. I can help you put a plan in place that will work to get you where you want to go. The key is to take that advice and follow through on your designed plan of action.

I've been very successful in what I do. For the past two years, I have been nominated as a finalist for the Mortgage Broker of the year as a company and as an individual broker. This is a tremendous accomplishment; to be recognized as one of the best of thousands of mortgage professionals all across Canada from British Columbia to Newfoundland. And it all started with some simple steps that I now also teach to my little girl as I help her to build her financial future.

My husband and I are a great match with our philosophies about money. He's more conservative and I have been the one to take a little more risk in investing. We balance each other out coming to a place of compromise on how and where we invest our money. With that balance, our future is bright.

I'm grateful for what I learned at a very young age. It has helped me to build a life of integrity around money and credit. I'm able to share knowledge that will help others to qualify for mortgages using what I know. It's so rewarding to see those years of learning bring brightness into the lives of new homeowners.

It is essential to master the art of moving forward regardless of your present circumstances. Even though it may not be easy now, know that day after day people push through those times to achieve their goals. The key is…you have to really want it. The resilience and persistent attitude and spirit of my mother has and continues to inspire me. Watching her overcome incredible challenges has made me strong and I am a better person in all aspects of my life; my job and my relationships with friends and family.

With persistence, knowledge, lessons learned and a good attitude, you too can achieve your dreams of success.

ABOUT THE AUTHOR

Anne Brill brings over twenty-five years of experience in the Financial Services industry; leveraging her expertise and know-how.

Anne began her career in banking in 1990. In 2001, she left the bank and opened her own company, Think Tank Financial where over the years she has won numerous awards from Verico and DLC-Prestige.

After joining Centum Metrocapp Wealth Solutions Inc. in July 2012, Anne Brill received several prestigious awards from CENTUM Financial Group.

Ann has sponsored numerous community events over the years while establishing herself as one of the most well-known and sought after mortgage brokers by clients and lenders alike.

Contact Information:
Anne Brill
Centum Metrocapp Wealth Solutions
716 Gordon Baker Road, Unit 204A
Toronto, Ontario M2H3B4
Ph: 416-289-2224

CHAPTER 3

ANNE AND TIANA'S CANDID CONVERSATION ON MONEY

Anne and Tiana Brille

It's truly unbelievable how even short time frames change kids' perspective on life and money.

Just recently, while shopping with Tiana (eight and a half years old) I asked Tiana, "Do you want this?"

She replied, "How much does it cost?"

When I told her, she said, "Too much money Mommy, we will buy that next time."

I've taught her that others around her are not as fortunate as she is and they don't have as much stuff. That makes Tiana sad and she would like to share her stuff with them. From a young age Tiana has chosen gifts from a toy store to donate to a local charity.

Here is a conversation I had with my daughter about six months before what I have just described.

Anne: Tiana what does money mean to you?

Tiana: I think it's something you need to get what you need in life, because you need to buy food and you need to have a house; you need to pay rent; you need to pay bills for water, for lighting, for a lot of that stuff. Money is pretty important.

Anne: Do you want to have money?

Tiana: It would be good to have a lot of money.

Anne: Why's that?

Tiana: Because when you're retired you don't want to be working. You don't want to be forced to work, so you want to have a lot of money aside so when you're retired you can just relax.

Anne: Do you think it's important to get a really good job to make more money?

Tiana: Yes then you could do more of what you want in life.

Anne: What do you think about saving?

Tiana: You really want to save because if you're forced to work when you're like 90 it's just not right. You would have to be homeless or still work when you're 90.

Anne: Do you know anything about credit?

Tiana: Not really.

Anne: Credit is... Well, it's like if you want to buy something and I loaned you a dollar but you had to give me back the dollar, that's called credit and I'm giving you credit.

Tiana: So it's like a loan.

Anne: Exactly. Are loans good?

Tiana: They are usually pretty good unless someone tries to scam you!

Anne: True. How much do you think is a lot of money?

Tiana: $50.00

Anne: That is a lot. What can $50.00 buy you?

Tiana: I don't know. There are not a lot of good things with $50 and there aren't a lot of bad things with $50. It's kind of decent.

Anne: What do you want to be when you grow up?

Tiana: A musician?

Anne: Are you going to go to University?

Tiana: Probably!

Anne: Who is your mentor? Who do you look up to?

Tiana: I don't know.

Anne: Taylor Swift?

Tiana: I don't know.

Anne: What's the most important thing for mommy's life?

Tiana: To make good money and to be able to live the life you want to have.

Anne: Is family important?

Tiana: Yes

Anne: Family comes first and money comes second. We all need money to survive.

Tiana: Well it's more that you can be pretty reckless with the money and when you're broke you can't buy what you need, like food. You need food to live.

Anne: Do you want to drive a nice car when you're older?

Tiana: Probably!

Anne: What kind of car do you like?

Tiana: A Ferrari

Anne: It's a lot of money

Tiana: I'm guessing it's like $30,000.

Anne: It's more so $300,000.

Tiana: $300,000?

Anne: That's a lot of money, so you'll have to make a lot of money to afford that! What else do you know about money?

Tiana: Well depositing money in the bank, because you can't have it on you all the time because someone can come up to you and mug you. They can take your $1,000 off you. They can take your wallet and take everything. It's always good to have a little bit of money and not a lot of money on you. It's good to have $100.00. That would be good to have.

Anne: Do you know what a debit card is?

Tiana: It's something you use to buy stuff and it goes right from your bank account. It goes to whatever you're buying or whatever store you're at or a restaurant and it gives them the money to put towards the purchase. So it goes to them and that gives them the money they need.

Anne: How about a credit card?

Tiana: I think it's pretty much the same thing. Like an American Express or Visa. They are pretty much all the same thing. There is not a lot of you can do with money except buy things. It's important, what you buy with the money because you want to be happy in life.

Anne: What makes you happy in life?

Tiana: My dog, my family, my friends. Things like that.

Anne: Does money make you happy?

Tiana: It's really what I can get from the money. Having money, it's not really something that you would have a lot of. It would be good to have. You can buy whatever you want, so it's good to have for that. Money is just a piece of paper pretty much it is just something that is made out of copper or iron. It is just a coin. It is just a bill, but the use of it is really good for buying stuff.

Anne: What does money mean to you?

Tiana: I already said it already because it's just a piece of paper. It's just metal. What I learned about money is it that it depends on what kind of bill it is. It could be $100 bill or a $50 bill or a $10 bill they all have different values and you can buy different things with them.

Anne: Do you want to have money when you grow up?

Tiana: Yes because then you can make your life even better. Why wouldn't you want to have a big house?

ABOUT THE AUTHOR

At just eight years old, Tiana is a yellow belt in Tae Kwan Do. She has played piano for two and a half years - guitar for two years and drums for a year and a half. She has even performed with a band at a local pub During her most recent performance, she sang Bad Blood by Taylor Swift and played drums. She has been the goalie on her soccer team for five years.

For the last six month, Tiana has been enjoying horseback riding. She loves animals, especially dogs. She is also very computer literate and has even up-loaded seven you tube videos that she personally performed in. Tiana is also a very strong swimmer. This young lady's interests and abilities are quite diverse!

She has won several Achievement Awards in school; the latest award is for Honesty. She has also won a Sharing Award. When she grows up Tiana wants to be famous and rich.

CHAPTER **4**

CREDIT: THE NEW SOCIAL STATUS

Gayle D'Haesseleer

When I turned 16, I knew I wanted a car. The last of 4 children, my parents had a pretty good "read" on what enabled children to NOT be successful. So by the time I came around, they totally knew what didn't work with kids. One thing they learned to do was to make sure that no money was ever given without earning it, and another was to make sure the kids understood the value of having to motivate themselves to earn money to get what they wanted. Consequently, I was compelled to work for a few years, part-time, while going to high school in order to fund the things they did not (or would not) provide for me, such as clothes, travel, gas, cars, etc.

I paid for my first car, a powder blue 1966 Ford Mustang in cash, $300 bucks. I ran it till it stopped and it was time for a new car. I went to my parents to ask to borrow the money. My father suggested that I go to the neighborhood credit union downtown to see what it would take for me to get a small loan for a used VW Karman Ghia I had spotted on a car lot. While I had a steady stream of income, I didn't have all the money required to pay for the car upfront. At seventeen, this was my first adult experience with any sort of a bank. When I asked for money, having already spent my paycheck, my parents used this teachable moment to deny the request (because how are you going to pay for something without the money?) and explain how credit works.

Everyone dealt in cash in those days since this occurred before any type of remote banking was possible. I walked downtown to the Credit Union and asked what it would take for me to borrow the amount required to buy a car. I was told to open a savings account, which I did. After making an application for a loan to buy the car, I was granted the loan, but not before promising to keep a certain amount of money in the savings account from which my car payments would be drawn automatically. When I got paid, I deposited my paycheck, less the amount of money I had decided I needed to live on and as agreed, made sure there was enough left there to make the payment.

Not realizing this was a form of budgeting, it might have been a good time for my parents to talk about that process! It would have been a great teaching opportunity for them to praise me for the correct behavior and to show me that what I was doing would help me later in life, if I kept it up. Apparently, they felt the experience alone taught me the lesson. When I decided to move to Florida I sold the car and paid off the loan! My first credit experience earned an A+.

Receiving a credit card at 20 years old was an ego boost! I thought I was the queen because the vendor thought enough of me to give me a $1,000 credit limit. Back then, there wasn't the same information available as there is today to credit seekers and credit providers. I knew nothing about the process. There was no scoring and monitoring or the credit bureaus that we have now. I could see where it would be entirely possible to spend away! It did not occur to me to think about how or even if I was able to pay back the credit line. After using the card then getting the bill, I realized how enticing this deal was and how it might not be easy for some people (including myself) to pay back what was spent! The bigger realization was that if I did not pay the bill in full, at the appropriated time, I would end up paying 17% interest on the balance. In all honesty...who can do that and feel good about it?

Probably one of my biggest tests of raising responsible children was our response to the use of money. Our respect of the power of money and how we talked about it in our home has effected how our children use money. We made it a subconscious process. Instead of it springing upon them in the post college credit card debt experience, talking to them rationally as they grew up and easing them into the knowledge of how money works created a straight forward "matter-of-fact" approach. By teaching them about earning, borrowing and paying back money, the concept of good credit and their increased worth would get them great results and better treatment.

These conversations happen regularly with my kids. In our family of 6, our kids were a black hole into which money was thrown. We are in a constant dialogue of how money is being spent. We included the family at the kitchen table when we paid our bills and allocated money. We taught budgeting, setting goals for which money was required, planning and saving to meet those goals. We teach value and deferred gratification. We monitor our own credit scores many times a year because they are a direct reflection of our ability to predict where and what we have available to us and how it will be used. We encourage our family to do the same.

The way we started with our kids was to explain that everyone from whom we borrow tells a credit agency how well we did paying them back. It is kind of like a report card on creditworthiness. The cool thing is we started when our kids are toddlers. As they grew we felt it essential, to talk about our cars, homes and lifestyle and how they are all affected by the strength of our credit score. Through the years, we have taught them that credit is a powerful tool to increase buying power and cash flow when used correctly. We have also done our best to impress upon them the consequences of not using that tool properly and that it is essential to be conscious as well as conscientious when goal planning and purchasing. Our kids saw the differences in our "stuff" compared to their friends' "stuff". Their friends might have had a bigger house or a more expensive car and we used those times as great conversation opportunity to introduce the concept of access to money, who might have earned it, budgeting and the role good credit plays in the process. As our kids got older, the explanation got more detailed as they grasped the idea of responsible money management.

Budgeting is one of the most comprehensive teaching tools my husband and I have used in our children's lives. While sitting at the kitchen table, Mom and Dad can, in a reasonable tone, talk and plan their monthly spending based on the money that is coming in and decide what will be spent in the future. Borrowing is a calculated risk. As our kids watched us during our money management process and experienced how much time and energy it takes to pay back debt, they were and continue to be more diligent about managing their money, having now more of a chance at financial success. If plans are made that require more money, then lifestyle is adjusted or not. There is always a choice. To be able to "see" the financial landscape is empowering. Proper use of the amazing tools we have available to us can provide so much in the way of security. Not knowing can be disastrous. This is always a place I start when consulting with my clients. I take them through the landscape of their business, showing them new ways to manage money so that people who they want to do business with view them as trustworthy; their financial future is thus assured.

Managing our reputation through credit scoring is surprisingly important. Creditworthiness has tentacles that reach deep into our daily lives. It is a full reflection of the people we are. We are judged by it. When I walked in to inquire about wireless service it was a piece of cake to get it. However, as part of their process, the wireless carriers check the credit score. Cell phones are readily available to those with good credit and can be obtained easily. For those with not so good credit or no credit, it is not easy at all. It may require up front deposits or pay in advance contracts until such time that one's creditworthiness is proven.

Premiums and qualifying for homeowner, car and even health insurance are generally determined by the condition of your credit. Coverage may be denied based on creditworthiness. This has direct impact on how we live our daily lives. The cost of buying or renting a home can have direct consequences if you haven't realized the importance of maintaining a good credit history. Landlords can deny you and banks will not open their doors to you. Rates are higher and higher for people who don't play the credit game well and the ones who need credit most actually end up paying so much more than they can afford just to get by. What lessons are they passing down to their kids?

The last time I went to buy a car at the VW dealership, after reviewing my application for credit, the salesman came back and asked me if I would like 2 new vehicles? Puzzled, I looked at him, he smiled and said, "You have stellar credit. You are golden! Choose anything you like!!"

I am lucky. Life taught me these lessons and I thrived well through having great mentors.

In the money world, walking your talk and following good money practices is key to getting the trust and recognition that leads to wealth and abundance on every level; even from people you've never met but only know you from your credit score!

ABOUT THE AUTHOR

Gayle Packard D'Haeseleer, compelling speaker, investor, author, personal and business strategy consultant is a leading authority in taking the deep dive into getting what you want.

Gayle's mission is to bring financial education to the masses and provide a clear path to saving time, effort and money, using specific tools, events and information platforms. She brings clarity and focused vision, peeling away the layers that cloud what you want. Her teachings will profoundly impact your life. Gayle will cut to the chase and let you know if you are barking up the wrong tree in your personal and business relationship with money.

Married for almost 30 years to Ron, Gayle has a combined family of 6 children and a bunch of grandchildren. She really loves to find a diamond in the rough.

To connect with Gayle, please email her at gayledhaeseleer@gmail.com, or visit her website at www.thewisdomsociety.com and find her book, *"I Always Drink When I Drive: And Other Ways Humans Sabotage Their Success"* on Amazon.com.

CHAPTER 5

LISTENING TO THE VOICE WITHIN

Patricia Karen Gagic

Once upon a time, someone said "Oh, Patricia! You are so brave to take on such a big job as a Bank Manager." At the time I was in my early twenties and those words never entered my mind. I was determined to work my way up the Corporate ladder and live in the Ivory Tower of banking. With discipline, much hard work and "guts" the reality took hold and shortly before my twenty fifth birthday the announcement was made and I became a "Branch Manager". The duties involved lending to both individuals on a personal level and corporate businesses.

The key element clients have when they walk through the door seeking financial assistance is "vision". Everyone has one! For some people their vision is to buy a new home or car. They see their future changing as they begin to prospect on what life will be like when they move ahead. This is where common sense should play a big role. However, for some who are less realistic about their lives and plans, disappointment can ensue. Vision provides hope and most often the incentive to make concrete changes in one's attitude toward spending and saving. If the desired outcome requires a down payment in order for financing to be approved, every effort should be made to budget and streamline the lifestyle to facilitate stuffing the golden piggy bank! Yes, it's true some financial institutions offer 100% financing, but before you jump in with both feet take a few moments to mindfully think through the pros and cons. Perhaps depreciation might eat up potential profit or least good case, the payment load might just be too overwhelming!

Humans are amazing creatures who often choose to say "yes" first and figure things out later. In the case of finances though, this might be the time to say "no" first. Too often we are driven by emotion as our desires can overshadow the real complexities of what we seem driven to acquire. A few months down the road when bills are adding up and the same revenue stream exists, the pressure can be significant. It is during these moments we sit back and say "Oh I wish I did not buy this or that! If only I had waited, saved more money and been patient!" What can the result lead to? Yes, low credit ratings, rejection for consolidation and sometimes unfortunately major stress and emotional chaos. Too often financial burdens are the root for many people to suffer depression, illnesses and deteriorating relationships at home and work.

The heart often rules the head when it comes to finances. This is where we can be undermined by the foibles of human nature. People have feelings and perceptions which sometime dictate their responding with emotion instead of reason. If we could harness our energy and visualize our goals through planning we might reduce the risk of potential suffering.

It is not easy to want something so much that you put the egg timer on yourself. Think before you push yourself into "I want it and I will do anything I can to get it now!" If only you could stop and take a moment to reflect on what this might bring to your next days ahead. Ask your wisdom self to kick in and spend a few minutes paying attention to all of the factors before you leap in with joy and jump out with regrets. Set up a strategy for yourself and make yourself a priority.

It is such a great feeling to have a vision and make a realistic plan to achieve your goal. The fun in planning should be equally as enjoyable as the final outcome. One of the memorable lines that boaters often quote is "The two happiest days of my life… The day I bought my boat and the day I sold my boat!" A fond memory surfaces for myself. As proud owners of a small cottage in Northern Ontario we made an emotional purchase of a beautiful boat. Yes, we were thrilled to take ownership and promptly arrived to the Marina with camera in hand. What we did not possess …"boating skills".. ZERO! After a five-minute crash course in mechanics we were on our own to navigate across the lake to our cottage. With incredible nervousness we managed our way however, saw a lovely little bridge and decided to detour. Well, the rocks were generously hungering for our less than cautious choice and delicately enjoyed chewing up our propeller. Welcome common sense and less emotion to save yourself from a lot of discomfort!

I recall a few decades ago meeting with a client who was a self-employed entrepreneur. He was incredibly excited to visit me and quickly closed my office door. He handed me an envelope which contained a check for One Million dollars. My client had won a lottery! Considering this was in 1979 this was considered a significant winning. The first thing he said to me was "My dreams are coming true!" Without hesitation I asked him, "What do you want to do with this? Are you interested in securing the principal to generate an investment income stream for the future? Perhaps donate some of the proceeds to a charity, friends or family?" His answer surprised me as he wanted to use the money to build a "dream home". All of it. During our conversation he revealed his childhood vision of living in a castle. The vision was embedded in his mind and this winning was clearly sufficient for him to build it.

What I learned and took from the gentleman was his strong passion and dedication to pursue his dreams. He actually had a plan. He shared with me that the reason he became an engineer was to generate a higher level of income, so that one day through his hard work and savings he would hire an Architect to design his dream home. He had always been organized, somewhat frugal, but most of all he was patient. Yes, he might have gone into debt years earlier to move forward on this, but the joy for him, was in the process. Each month he and his wife would marvel at how much they had saved without ever feeling they were striving or depriving themselves. They simply distinguished between what mattered in their world. The universe had smiled upon and gifted him with a lucky break. His patience had been rewarded.

Of course, this is not the usual outcome for people who have a vision. It is a fair and good reminder of how laying the groundwork, following through with a flexible but committed strategy can save heartache in the future of one's financial life. The greatest prospect of success will be achieved when implementation with a bit of patience and calming of emotion rules. Yes, the castle no matter what form it takes can be yours!

As I reflect on my own journey through the myriad of credit decisions I have made, there is one emotion I will always acknowledge and feel well disposed to have. There is gratefulness. From the first moment I negotiated with my parents right up to the large corporate loan I sought for my business, I am always thankful. It is so easy to assume "credit is just there!".... We live in a society where access and benefit are immediate. We live in a country of privilege. What I realize is how often we take privilege for granted. We need to remind ourselves how blessed we are to have these rights.

Imagine living in a society where mortgage companies don't exist. Can you comprehend the complexity of building a home without the assistance of a lender? How many years would it take to save for the first home if one had to pay in cash? Yes, from our cars, furniture, homes, luxury items we are beneficiaries of a society with privilege. I would ask you to stop and pause for a moment. Think about your family, generations before you and what life might have been like. Some of us come from distant and foreign lands where systems are not in place to support our "visions".

Life, with all of its ups and downs, teaches us many lessons. We celebrate the tiniest of achievements to epic moments, whereas the reality is that the world around us is forever changing.

Life is impermanent. Embracing each day is a discipline for a positive life and we need to practice this. We do live in a very diverse world and there are times when our mental, moral and intellectual differences can bring us together, or set us apart. This does not change the fact we have the ability to make choices. When considering opportunities, I urge you to be mindful. Think about whether your choice is one that may have long term ramifications. Will the consequences of your choice provide you with a positive outcome?

During a very turbulent time in the early 1990's when interest rates were outrageously high, investors walked down very narrow pathways. Some were able to benefit by their strategic wise choices while others did not sustain their actions positively and fell by the wayside.

They say history repeats itself. If we are to learn anything from our previous decision, it might be to simply pay attention in a particular way. We all desire to have pleasure and happiness throughout our lives. I remember listening to people share their personal misfortunes and triumphs with intense curiosity towards their attitude. It was remarkable to see the differences! Some were groveling in self-pity, declaring their losses as tsunami's, while others said "I live in the now, I cannot change what has happened, only move forward!" A lot of this rubbed off on me and in times when I was less resilient, I would quickly clear myself of those negativities and smile, knowing I was still capable of fulfilling my vision. Yes, it is very challenging to be unattached to less favorable outcomes, however it allows the creation of a new vision to take place...if you give it life.

It takes one second to change our minds. We do it all the time.

If you feel that the vision you are manifesting is achievable, then allow yourself to dream big with the added bonus of your own wisdom. Pay attention to the little red flags that flirt their shiny glow in your mind's eye when perhaps something just does not seem to add up. We all have intuition. It's a sense, a knowing, a gut feeling that we need to pay attention to, sharpening our inner listening skills; especially when we are in negotiation for our "dreams." There is always room to take some time until the right "one" comes along. It takes courage sometimes to walk away from something we feel so much attachment to. In the long run if you give yourself permission to create patience with a dribble of wisdom, the outcome may be more favorable than you expect. My dream and vision is for everyone to find peace within and make better choices resulting in excellence. Give yourself permission to dream rich! And open your heart to financial freedom.

One of my favorite quotes is by Ralph Waldo Emerson.

"Without a rich heart, wealth is an ugly beggar".

ABOUT THE AUTHOR

In 2015 Patricia Gagic was named one of WXN Top 100 Most Powerful Women in Canada in the BMO Arts and Communications category. In 2013, she was recognized by the International Order of St. George and Knighted as a Dame of the Order. Patricia is an accomplished International Contemporary Artist, an Award winning Author and entrepreneur. She is represented by BB International Fine Arts in Switzerland exhibiting in Europe and North America.

Patricia is a Certified Meditation Specialist/Facilitator in Applied Mindfulness, Transformative Mindfulness and Mindfulness without Borders from the University of Toronto. Also a Feng Shui Level 3 Consultant and Reiki Master, Patricia is a member of the Ontario Cabinet for the Friends of the Canadian Museum for Human Rights and Board member of the Sir Edmund Hilary Foundation. Patricia is nominated for Woman of the Year, YMCA Peace Medal and recipient of the Award of Excellence Toronto Women's Expo. She is Ambassador to Friends to Mankind and Project Cambodia.

Learn more about Patricia by visiting her website at www.inspiredtoberewired.com

CHAPTER **6**

BUILDING THE DREAM AND LIVING IT THROUGH - THE POWER OF POSITIVE CREDIT

Patricia Giankas

I was nineteen years old and I had just delivered my first child. Having lived a sheltered life, I was clueless about how to care for a child. When my daughter was born I was very ill with chicken pox. The baby was isolated and had to remain in an incubator after I was released from the hospital. With a heavy heart, I went home. I was not able to see my baby for a week; the hospital was two hours away from my residence and there was a transportation strike, I would have to ride the bus to the hospital. The doctors also didn't want me to go to the hospital because I was still contagious with chicken pox. I was still recovering from a very high fever and those stubborn little swellings were everywhere on my body. I loved my little girl, and was excited when she finally came home to a newly sterilized home. It was 1974.

My husband worked days and I worked evenings. I had to return to work after three months maternity leave. I was fortunate to find a friend who lived down the street who also just had a baby. She took care of my daughter for a couple of hours in between our shifts. I would come home at 10 PM, make dinner for the next day, sterilize the baby's bottles and prepare whatever she would need for the following day. I would also do whatever house work needed to be done. I was exhausted. The next day I did it all over again.

We had very little money at the time and I wanted a house so badly I could taste it. So, I made a plan to get what I wanted. I sold Tupperware, Avon and Coppercraft to make extra cash. On my day off from my regular job, I worked part time at a store. In a short time I advanced from sales clerk to accounting clerk. I was focused on earning money to buy that house.

My daughter was my absolute joy. I used to run, not walk, but run the half mile home so I could have time with her, before she would go to sleep for the night. I kept my goal of buying a house in front of me and worked hard, yet I still made time to be with my children. Now we were a family of four with my son's arrival in 1976. We moved to a larger apartment but I knew we wouldn't stay there too long.

It was tough trying to balance my life, especially with a husband who had no patience for kids. I had them fed, bathed and ready for bed every night. Through many challenges, we strove for a better life. We did whatever was necessary. I was back in school and every exam I passed put me one step closer to the top. Life got easier. I kept up with my school work and took a job at a bank. Each year, I was promoted until I became a branch manager. I must say, I learn real fast.

Having the goal of buying a house kept me going, even when I felt a little down. I would remember my goal of buying a house and in 1978, having saved $25,000 for a deposit, I officially became a homeowner! Fortunately, I was able to bring my parents to Canada to help me out with the kids. My dad left status, a prominent job and a gorgeous home; they sacrificed a lot for me and my children so I could live and build my dream. I am forever grateful to them. Knowing that the kids were in Mom's care took a great deal of stress from me. Today as a grandmother myself, I try to pay that forward by doing the same for my daughter and my grandchildren.

Even with great responsibility at home, having small children to care for, I did it! I bought that house for $67,000. I got a 10.25% interest rate and paid it off in 5 years. My third child, my pleasant surprise was born right after the house was paid off in 1984.

During those years I grew up quickly, having a clearer understanding of life. Then reality struck home. I opened my eyes one morning and suddenly realized that the person I was married to for 18 years was a complete stranger. We had no debts, no mortgage, and we had money in the bank. The kids were getting older and I was winning awards climbing the corporate ladder, but I had no one to share it with. It was time to wake up! Before I knew it, I was divorced. (1986) I took complete responsibility for all of the choices I had made, resolving to make the most of it. Ironically my now ex-husband reentered my life two years later.

After his return, I literally tore my house down and built a "monster home." We only lived in that house for two months after friends and family helped us to complete it when the building contractor disappeared with $200,000. Materials he had purchased with that money to build our house, were being put into other homes he had contracted. I have actually lived to watch that contractor lose everything, having not done the right thing. He has since been divorced and lives in a basement apartment. Can you say Karma?? If I had only known, I would never have done business with him.

How does something like this happen, you ask? I had been working at the bank and I took out a Construction Financing Loan. Here's how a Construction loan works:

A construction loan is underwritten to last for only the length of time it takes to construct the home (about 12 months on average), and you are essentially given a line of credit up to a specific limit. You submit "draw requests" to your lender and only pay interest as you go. There are no prepayment penalties, because the amount loaned for construction will be paid off with a final mortgage loan.

Normally the bank will release funds to pay the contractor based on completion of the work as the construction progresses. What ended up happening with my loan? The bank had given me all the financing up front instead of releasing it according to the draw schedule as the work was being completed. When the contractor asked for the money, I gave it all to him after he threatened to walk off the job saying that it was necessary for him to buy all the materials at once. I handed him the money fully believing that he would use that money to purchase all the materials and complete my house. Instead, he took the money and used it to build and complete all the neighboring homes. All of the materials for those homes were actually delivered to my house and then the contractor would move the material to whichever job site he wanted to use it on. I only found out this was going on when I realized that even though the neighborhood was starting to look good, nothing was being done at my house.

Excuses of his wife leaving him, and needing to spend time at home with her and the family eventually led to the contractor not showing up on the job at all. After 6 months, I had to enlist the financial help of family and friends to get the house completed. There were lots of tears sitting in that house. During the completion of the house, the stress was too much for our renewed relationship to survive; having my ex-husband back in my life was not working. So I bought him out and kept the house.

I couldn't sell the house because property values had already tumbled down. Because of all the issues associated with it, I really didn't want to stay in that house, so in 1990 I ended up renting it to another family and I moved into a rental apartment. There was just too much hurt in that house for me to stay there.

Shortly thereafter, I purchased another home as a rental property. During this time, I met my now husband of 26 years and together we purchased a home where we lived with our blended family. In the span of 10 years after that, because I now understood the value of credit and finances, I was able to purchase 5 rental properties. I never made a late payment, or acquired any credit card debt during that time.

In 1994 I worked for a U.S. loan and finance company in Canada giving small loans at 32% interest rate with an APR of not more than 39%. New immigrants, lower income families wanting to improve their lives, yet barely making ends meet came to us for short term financing, which broke my heart. From that, I found a way to educate these clients on how they could increase their credit, which would then open the door for much better interest rates from the banks to pay the higher interest loans off.

Understanding what financial freedom means, I became passionate about educating people on how to manage their finances, build their credit scores and live a better life. During the year 2000 I owned my own mortgage company with approximately two hundred mortgage agents working in that company. I encountered so many people who wanted to buy their first home, and were unable to do so because they had tarnished credit. There were also many people who couldn't afford to buy because they had been unable to properly budget their money.

In today's world, many families get into financial trouble without even realizing the effect credit cards and unsecured loans have on their lives. Most don't understand the ramifications of getting deep into bad debt. Many times, these credit seekers find themselves taking cover under the bankruptcy laws, then needing six or seven years to recover from that decision.

In 2005, I created a workbook "Managing Your Money and Understanding Credit" which taught the concepts of budgeting and cash flow. People could now take a detailed look at their individual situations and make changes and choices accordingly. Anyone who used this workbook course earned a certificate of accomplishment when they finished. During this time, I also became a bankruptcy insolvency counselor so that I could help my clients who had overextended themselves with bad debt. I was able to coach them on the ramifications of negative credit while helping them learn about and understand positive credit. We found solutions that would keep them out of bankruptcy and rebuild their financial lives. Ultimately the goal was for them to become proud homeowners again.

Then in 2012, I was introduced to Rusty Bresse in Atlanta, Georgia, who is also a contributor to this book. He created the Score Navigator software that he talks about in his chapter. We took all the knowledge from the previous companies and created an interactive, easy to use online product; **Score-Up** was born. This software allows people to have even more insight and control of their credit. It's easy to understand and simple to follow, showing you how to increase your score in 60 days or less. Try it for yourself by visiting www.scorenavigator.com.

Our company gives people a choice. We educate families, allowing them to have a better understanding when making decisions about debt. There must be a balance and a plan in place when borrowing money to achieve your goals. Our system gives our clients that balance. We help people attain their long and short term financial goals while avoiding financial pitfalls and building wealth.

In today's society, most people are not well informed as to the importance of their credit score. I believe there are several reasons for this:

- No discipline
- Language barriers
- Peer pressure
- Lack of education
- Downturn in the market
- Lack of understanding of what it means to "budget"
- Reduced income/ same expenses
- Divorce
- Gambling
- Underemployment
- Medical expenses
- Banking on a windfall
- Financial illiteracy
- No money communication skills
- Saving too little or not at all
- Poor money management

In the past, credit card companies would increase a credit limit without the cardholder's consent. The average consumer loved this because it gave them more "buying power," and buy they did! There was no recognition that the "buying power" was not money. They would indeed have to pay the credit card balance. This process didn't take into consideration the actual capability of the cardholder to make the payments and maintain good credit. In today's credit environment, the credit card companies do not increase credit limits without the consent of the cardholder and requalifying them for the increase in credit line based on the merits of their application.

As a rule, most people don't plan ahead. We all must learn to do this, not only to plan ahead for our monthly expenses, we must plan ahead for our future expenses and for retirement.

Once someone loses their credit status, it takes time and money to recover from that. As fear sets in, people tend to just set the issue aside, and then let it go since it's easier than the effort it would take to resolve. Then denial sets in. Buying power becomes a thing of the past, and thus the beginning of paycheck to paycheck living, which is really not living, it's barely survival.

Embarrassed to go to the bank because there is either money owed to the bank, or the decision was made to seek help under bankruptcy protection, hoping that the whole situation would just go away, people feel stuck in their financial mess. Many people have this idea that the bank teller or customer service representative will look down on them and some people begin to fall into to the extremes of paranoia and depression. Some consider losing their credit to be a "death" of sorts, and can actually go into a period of mourning. Some mourn longer than others. Some do not have, nor do they understand that there are tools they can use to move forward.

In the meantime, what are we teaching our kids? Our children watch and learn from everything we do. There comes a time when we have to look at how this is affecting everyone around us and look for a fresh start.

LET'S START OVER!

It's not your fault.

You did the best you could with what you had, both in money and in knowledge. When the financial aspect of life gets stressed, families start to play the blame game. Of course, no one wants to take responsibility for the financial situation the family is in. This can get rough with things like verbal confrontations and abuse, and sometimes it gets physical. What good does any of this do? None. People forget that they got into this mess together and they can certainly work it through together. There are tools available to them.

Sometimes it takes the kids to bring us to our senses.

When they are unable to "keep up with the Joneses" with brand name clothing and school gear, they could potentially become victims of bullying in school. If that's the case, they tend to shut down and feel "not good enough" among their peers, succumbing to the pressure. School should be a "safe haven," but in this day and age, it seems that is a thing of the past. How has your financial situation affected your kids? We should not be concerned about our kids wearing the designer clothes, but we should impress up on them to take of what they do have, also making sure that they have the books they need to excel regardless of what they are wearing, paying attention to the necessities of life. It's time to make a change!

Our certified credit coaches work with our clients, every step of the way, to rebuild their credit and bring their financial situation into the light so they can see what is necessary to achieve their financial goals. This program was designed to help eliminate financial stress in families from all walks of life. Our objective is for people to reclaim the responsibility of managing their credit and finances to reach their goals and live joyfully.

Score-Up's coaching program is similar to some of today's most recognized weight loss programs. From time to time people go on fad diets, looking for the easy fix. Then interest dwindles, or it becomes too difficult and the diet is over. However, when someone is seriously looking to make a long term change, they may go to a company where they have live coaches to help them every step of the way. The coach's job is to keep the client motivated to achieve their goal. It's like having a personal trainer. As you might conclude, the success rate is much higher when someone has a coach guiding them and cheering them on to the finish line.

Our system has many features which are designed to assist clients with their budgeting and the best use of funds. Some of the features are Long and Short term Recommendation to improve credit, Target Simulator and Money Simulator. Score-Up and the Score Navigator software also notifies the client when payment is due on their accounts and tells them which day of the month to make the payments. It gives them recommendations to improve their credit. There are "manage your money" modules available in our system to educate people so that they will not have to face this situation ever again, IF they make a plan and stick to it! Like the weight loss program we just spoke about, in order to achieve your goals, there is work to be done. Be diligent!

My motivation to help others comes partly from experience in my own personal life as described earlier with the contractor who ran off with the money and supplies for the house I had worked so hard to provide for my family. With that in mind, I decided I could do something to help young families. I would teach them about the value of their credit and manage their finances. It was nine years ago that I envisioned the creation of a software program that would help people to manage their credit like no other software out there.

For a long time, I spent every waking moment of my life thinking about how to make this happen. I'm not a software developer, so I needed someone to create the program that would make my idea become a working reality. The closest I was ever able to come to making this idea come alive on my own was to combine a couple of different software programs. When the time was exactly right, I met Rusty Bresse, who had software similar to what I had envisioned, so I pursued a conversation with the developer who lives in a small town in Georgia. Shortly after, Score-Up was born! What were the odds of this happening? I believe when we pursue something diligently and for the right reasons, the universe conspires in our favor. It certainly was the truth for Score-Up!

> *"Nothing comes ahead of its time, and nothing ever happened that didn't need to happen." ~Byron Katie*

Through many challenges, Relationally, Emotionally and Financially, (REF) I feel I have been given the opportunity and a wonderful gift to help others. I've actually become a REF of sorts through this process. I'm grateful to be on this journey despite all the obstacles. It's been incredibly rewarding to watch my ideas come to life and have an impact on the future of others. My team and I are doing our best to help people find financial peace.

ABOUT THE AUTHOR

 Patricia Giankas brings over thirty years of experience in the Financial Services industry; leveraging her expertise and know-how. She recognized the need for offering clients complete financial representation. Patricia has been recognized in her field of expertise and has established a reputation as the true expert and leader in the mortgage industry.

Committed to making a difference for others, Patricia has founded Silver Lining Healing Center which brings knowledge and service to those who are in need of support in managing their finances and resources. She is ever exploring ways that she can share her message of hope with people who are lost in today's financial difficulties.

Patricia has lectured at women shelters. She has provided assistance to community charities, bringing hope and help to various areas of the world. In this time where many people are turned upside down in their finances, Patricia helps them to make sense of their financial mess.

Connect with Patricia at p.giankas@score-up.ca.

CHAPTER 7

MATTHEW'S CONVERSATION WITH ME ABOUT MONEY

Patricia Giankas and Matthew Sulaman

It's really interesting to talk to kids about money. It's actually fun to talk with them about any part of life for that matter. I recently had a conversation with my grandson, Matthew. I would like to share it with you because it makes me giggle when I think about the simplicity and ease with which children share their feelings and youthful knowledge of life and how things work. Matthew is actually a very saavy little one; see for yourself.

Patricia: What is your name?

Matthew: Matthew Rodgers.

Patricia: Matthew, what can you tell me about money?

Matthew: Money is...It's about all kinds of stuff. It's about having a job. You have to pay to get your job anyways, so you have to save money where ever you find it. You find it on the airport floor, you have to pick it up if you want and you can use it. If you find it anywhere, you can use it to get a job and then you'll get more money. If you get money, you can get...If you have money and you don't like your house anymore, you can buy a new house. If you want a car, you can buy a car.

Patricia: If you don't have any money, what happens?

Matthew: Just use your own credit card.

Patricia: What if your credit card is full and you have no more room? What are you going to do?

Matthew: I don't know.

Patricia: No?

Matthew: Probably you just go to the bank, ask them if you could have another debit card and some money.

Patricia: Really, so a loan. Ask the bank for a loan?

Matthew: Yeah.

Patricia: What if the bank says no? What are we going to do?

Matthew: You have to convince them.

Patricia: Convince them?

Matthew: Yeah.

Patricia: How do you do that, baby?

Matthew: Just try something. Just try anything.

Patricia: Try anything like what?

Matthew: Try anything like asking them, "Please, please, I really want a job and a car."

Patricia: No, but you need money. You have to ask the bank for the money.

Matthew: If they say no, then just ask them again.

Patricia: What if everybody says no? What are we going to do? How are we going to buy groceries and live, and buy your toys?

Matthew: You have to grow some seeds, find someone that has all kinds of seeds like apple seeds, tree seeds, apple trees, and carrots, carrot seeds, and all kinds of seeds for food, and ask them if we could trade for something else, and then you can trade. Then you have food.

Patricia: Who taught you that? You take the seeds, plant them, you have some food.

Matthew: Well, you first have to wait for a long time.

Patricia: Oh, my gosh. What's going to happen until then?

Matthew: Just go around, walk around until you find a store, well, until you find some places that are free. If you find any stores, go into the store, see if anything is free and get it.

Patricia: There's a food bank that gives you food for free. Is that what you're talking about?

Matthew: Yes. Yes, there is. Yes. We can also get food stamps if we need food.

Patricia: How long are we going to be doing that? Don't you think it's important to have good credit, so you can go to the-

Matthew: Yeah, but that's what happens if you don't have money. Goodbye.

And the conversation is over at the will of a child.

What if life were that simple? No cares, just plant some seeds, get things for free simply by asking. In a way, that's what today's population is doing with their credit cards, acting like children without any concept of delayed gratification. There is a better way.

ABOUT THE AUTHOR

Matthew Sulaman is the grandson of Patricia Giankas and the love of her life. This seven year old is in second grade at a French Immersion School. He enjoys competitive swimming, Tae Kwon Do and playing chess. Minecraft and Legos, playing with his model/toy cars and collecting Pokemon cards are his hobbies. Matthew's favorite thing to do is spend time with his family and friends.

Matthew would love to be a policeman when he grows up and wants a Mustang to be his first car. He loves the outdoors, is participating as an Earth Ranger to help protect wildlife, and has encouraged his family to donate to protecting wildlife rather than buying birthday presents for him.

Matthew is a loving boy whose brilliance and kindness shine brighter each day. He is a giver of love, hope and genuine happiness to his family and friends. Matthew's future will be filled with greatness.

CHAPTER 8

CASH OR CHARGE, MR. RAMSEY?

Michael C. Griffin

I tried to rent a car the other day and my Visa card has expired. No big deal. I assumed I would just pay cash. Nope! The rental agent told me that cash was not accepted and a current valid and acceptable credit card was mandatory. Trying to calm the rising octaves in his broken English, I calmly produced an American Express card that I always held in reserve. Unfortunately, this did not solve the issue as I had anticipated. "No, no. American Express no good. Only Visa, only Master Card, American Express no good!!" Gathering what patience I had, I left.

Credit cards, credit bureaus, credit rating, good credit, no shirt, now shoes, no credit. How did we, as a civilized society wind up being held hostage by plastic cards and credit scores? For the answer to this question let us turn back the pages of financial history and discover the origin of these money eating monsters.

Let's begin with my grandfather. I remember papa sitting at the kitchen table railing against the consequences of going into debt!

"Never borrow a dime unless you want to pay quarter for it. JC Penny's never offered credit. Not while old James 'cash' Penny was alive, that is. Henry Ford knew the score. You couldn't buy a model A unless you paid cash for it. Now look at Ford. It's got the biggest credit department in the industry. People all over America are in hock up to their eye balls trying to pay off those old gas-guzzlers. Listen to me son; you can't spend yourself into prosperity or borrow your way outta debt."

My grandfather is long gone but I can still hear his words. He did not die a rich man but he did pay cash for his own funeral.

It's not easy to believe that credit cards have only been around since 1950. The first card was a piece of plastic called the Diner's Club Card that was the brain child of Frank McNamara so that New Yorkers could frequent select restaurants.

Then 1958 on the left coast, Bank of America issued the first Bank America card. Jumping on the credit wagon, a new company gives birth to American Express. Americans were captivated by the credit card and in 1976; Bank of America changed its card name to Visa. In 1989 Sears got into a dispute with Visa and issued their own cards called Discover. Sixty-five years ago credit was viewed as sinful. Now it is a way of life and seventy-seven percent of all adults have one or more cards with the average American holding seven plastic temptations. It is fair to say that in today's world we now have more credit cards in our sights than ducks in a shooting gallery. The question is who's the duck? My grandfather could tell you.

I'm sure we all remember our first credit card. Mine was a Master Card and she was a sexy temptress. We had a torrid love-loathe relationship for ten years. I say love- loathe because I loved to use her, but I loathed paying for it. My first experience was an emergency situation. I charged an airline ticket so I could fly up north to visit my mother in the hospital. Using my card was so easy I was able to rationalize its continuing use in the pursuit of personal pleasure. I think that is called the 'Drunken Sailor Syndrome.' I was able to convince myself I was building credit and not wasting my money on wine, women, and song.

There are none so in the dark as those who do not see the eighteen percent interest in the fine print. I actually believed I was a shrewd businessman by only paying the minimum payment. I was so naïve I tried to buy waterfront property in Florida with my Master Card. That was when I completely bottomed out. After that epitome I went cold turkey. I stopped eating out, buying the house drinks, and baubles for the babes.

Ten years after receiving my first credit card I got divorced; not from a woman, but from the attractive, addictive and demanding mate that was my credit card. Finally, through self-sacrifice and sheer will power I was debt free. I was ecstatic and my credit rating was an astounding 785. I was so charged-up and empowered with my own business acumen that I bought a house and signed a 150,000 dollar mortgage. Did I say debt free? Ha, ha, ha -oh my aching assets....

This brings us to the credit bureaus and that all important FICO or coveted credit score. It is not a measure of wealth or success. It is more of a measurement of how well you play the game of charge and pay. If you maintain valid accounts, use them regularly and pay at least the minimum amounts due with no delinquencies your score will improve. The longer and cleaner your track record, the higher your score will be with a maximum of 850. This does not mean you are rich or even solvent. It only means you pay your bills on time. In order to qualify for a home mortgage or other large purchase, a good fico score of 700 to 739 is visually required with some expectations. There are those companies that you can contact and for a small fee they will tell you your own credit score. They are Transunion, Experian and Equifax.

Conversely, if you have accumulated unsatisfactory debt or have a conflict, you can contact them and with the applicable mounds of paper work have the disputed items corrected. It is also good to be fluent in several languages and have a Philadelphia law firm on retainer.

This next segment I will call "Attack of the Haunted Credit Cards!" I know it sounds like a B movie horror flick, but unfortunately it is a true story and it happened to a good friend of mind.

Stan and Louanne got married in a fever. For the first several years of their marriage, everything went according to plan, including a new house surrounded by a white picket fence, and weekend Tupperware parties. They were the perfect couple pursuing the great American dream when the credit goblins came out to play! They are insidious little devils that have infested many an unwary household. Stan was pragmatic and plodding; never one to fall for the glitter or the glitz or a carnival barker. Louanne was the polar opposite. She loved her Harlequin books, her Hollywood magazine and shopping. She shopped for everything; specializing in

Longaberger baskets, Barbie dolls, and Beanie Babies. Louanne became increasingly dependent on her credit cards to feed her shopping addiction and her compulsion for collecting designer baskets, Barbies, and every Beanie ever made. She rented a P.O box to hide credit card bills and a storage unit to store her purchases. For several years life went on as usual, fortunately with no children then came that momentous day when the devil asked for his dues.

Early one morning Stan got a call from a collection agency asking to know if he could speak with Louanne about her overdue accounts. Once the credit cat was out of the bag it was a downhill slide into divorce court. Today Stan is still reeling from the loss of his house, his wife, and a healthy chunk of his income paying past due storage fees, attorney expenses, alimony and collection agencies.

Thankfully, not all stories end this way and millions of people use their credit cards responsibly. I believe that knowledge and discipline are two of the most important factors in keeping the credit cache comfortable and friendly. Please only allow yourself one (if you must) real credit card. I would suggest getting a debit card instead of a charge card. With a debit card you must back your purchase with money in the bank. If you choose to exercise your credit card, keep a record of the amounts so at the end of the billing cycle you can pay off the entire amount. Read and be aware of the consequences of not paying it off. Outstanding balances are subject to outrageous interest rates. At seventeen to twenty plus percent it doesn't take long for your lunch to disappear. Credit Card companies will offer you to pay only a tiny bit of what you owe so you may charge more and more and can snow ball yourself into a dark place. If you don't believe me, find Stan or Louanne and ask them.

For those unfortunate souls that find themselves behind the credit card eight ball (no, you cannot pay your Visa with your Master Card) seek help from someone with expertise in personal finance. A friend a family member, a financial advisor, or even an addiction counselor may be required to save you.

Another good friend of mine who I have known for many years has been through the credit gauntlet a number of times. Some of his stories are funny enough to be comedy club material. Nevertheless, each one of them teaches a real but not so funny lesson.

Harvey (not his real name) knew a deal when he saw one. He was in Lowes one day looking to buy an inexpensive gas grill when he learned of their new no interest – no minimum for eighteen months program. "Wow! Buy now and pay later," he thought to himself. Harvey couldn't wait to sign-up. He bought himself a brand new Mega Webber Combo. Part smoker, part Dutch oven, part bar-b-que with electric rotisseries for chicken and vegetables. A state of the art, computer programmed propane powered, kitchen – on – wheels extravaganza, for a paltry $ 2,995.00. Eighteen month later Harvey had only paid two hundred dollars toward the nut when suddenly his time was up and the balance plus the accrued interest at twenty-three percent came due. Harvey does not shop at Lowes any more but there is a picture of him towing his 'kitchen on wheels' into their parking lot behind his pickup truck on their website.

Harvey's next adventure into the wonderful world of clever marketing and snake oil salesmen occurred when he purchased two cars for the price of one.

What a deal! No credit check, no money down, no dealer fees, zero due at closing and zero percent financing. All of this with no hidden costs, unless you were able to find them written in legalese at the bottom of the page. Harvey went for it — hook, line, and sinker. Two new vehicles for the price of one luxury model. The deal was signed; Harvey got a shiny black compact and his wife a pretty rosy-red one.

Initially the monthly payment was $ 495.00 but when the small print detail came to light it soared to $ 545.00 the following year it skyrocketed to $ 635.00 to cover all those 'hidden' costs. Harvey couldn't manage the increase and fell behind. After a while he got further behind until he stopped paying anything.

One rainy morning his wife left the house early for work and was greeted with the horrifying specter of seeing both their cars being driven onto a flatbed truck and hauled away. To Harvey's fast thinking credit he was ready for her.

"It's okay honey. I wanted it to be a surprise; I traded those two lemons in on a new BMW for you and a cab is on the way. I'll pick you up after work in your new Beamer." Beautiful. Harvey had exactly eight hours to negotiate a deal on a new BMW. Today, Harvey and his wife are still happily married; although her 325i is getting a little old and his beat up VW bug has 300,000 miles on it.

During this discourse, I have shown how our society has become dependent on credit and how it can control or even really impact negatively our very lives. From personal experience and those of others, I have presented some basic principles that we can utilize in this wonderful but sometime not easy to navigate world of credit. Principals are important but there is no substitute for personal responsibility.

We live in an increasingly complex and competitive environment. It is incumbent on all of us to be constantly vigilant and to protect our credit, our finances and our families with every resource we have. In the immortal words of the thirty third president of the United States, Harvey's Truman, *"The buck stops here."*

ABOUT THE AUTHOR

Michael C Griffin is a retired airline captain and a Vietnam veteran. He is the author of Tales of the Lost Flamingo, a soon to be published novel, titled Tropical Knights, and a children's book due out in 2016.

Mr. Griffin is married and lives in Delaware and Florida.

CHAPTER 9

BEING THE PHOENIX

Kathryn A. Hathaway

I'm Kathryn Hathaway, and I'm a bankruptcy lawyer. We'll just get that out there in the beginning of this chapter. Some might say that I represent the antithesis of the theme of this book on great credit. Strangely enough, sometimes the fastest path from bad credit to good credit is by going through a bankruptcy to get to the other side. A Bible quote that supports this vision for me is *"Yea, though I walk through the valley of the shadow of death, I will fear no evil."* (Psalm 23) The key word in that sentence is "through."

My mission is to restore my clients to positive and constructive participation in the economy. People who are "buried in debt" are not able to participate in the economy. They can't purchase your widgets if all their income is being used up to pay credit card bills. If they have judgments against them and their income is being garnished, not only are they unable to buy your widgets, they often lose the will to work and they quit their jobs, contenting themselves with unstable jobs or working "under the table." This does not constitute a positive participation in the economy. They aren't buying your widgets or anyone else's for that matter.

I've been supporting clients in letting go of their negative financial pasts and saving their houses for over 25 years. I love what I do. I've never believed, however, that it is enough to just clear debt, so I also help clients to rebuild their credit and their lives after bankruptcy. For years I've been teaching clients about the next steps to take after they've gotten the fresh start bankruptcy is supposed to give. Together we build a new dream. We plan changes to their budgets, design credit rebuilding plans, and make a plan to save for the future. When the clients are entrepreneurs, we strategize how to revitalize their businesses.

I recently received an email from a client that affirmed I was on the right track (and also made my day):

Mrs. Hathaway,

Good morning. I wanted to follow up with you on something. 5 years ago I came into your office with my tail tucked between my legs. To say that I was scared and embarrassed would be an understatement. The last 4 years I have followed and done everything you have told me to do. I got a new job which I shared with you and have been at this job for now over 4 years. I have built a pretty decent IRA, a pretty respectable savings account and have an updated credit score of 700. And last but not least I am finally closing on my new home next week I wanted to share a picture with you to let you know my progress. Had it not been for you taking the time to meet with me and assist me with this and guide me in the right direction I don't know what I would have done or where I would be right now.

THANK YOU FROM THE BOTTOM OF MY HEART!!!

John T

John's message came just at the right time to encourage me in my new endeavor – Being the Phoenix: Inspiration Education and Tools for Rising from the Ashes of Financial Ruin! This Phoenix "rises" from my desire to share a new mindset, method and way of manifestation to create a prosperous and abundant future after bankruptcy with a wider audience of people than just my own clients.

Filing bankruptcy is not a reflection of who you are. It is a tool that can help you to start anew. It only means that what you were doing and thinking in the past wasn't working to create a prosperous and abundant future. You might be someone who could have benefited from financial education that might have led to making great financial decisions. Fortunately, you can change your thinking and actions to create something different in the future. Being the Phoenix, LLC has some great tools to help you do just that. Visit me at www.bethephoenix.net.

What's the effect of bankruptcy on a credit score? Most of my clients arrive in my office with credit scores in the 400's or the low 500's. Their credit reports are littered with "Late pays" "No pays" and "Charge offs."

Often they had just tried to finance a car or refinance their house and were told that they should just file bankruptcy and start over. In fact, lenders are a primary referral source for me. If the client's credit score is already really low, bankruptcy may actually be a positive solution.

As projected by a credit report vendor I use, if the client's credit score is in the 400's or low 500's, it is not uncommon for the projected score 15 months after bankruptcy discharge to be as much as 130 points higher. If you file a bankruptcy when your score is 680, on the other hand, filing bankruptcy will likely make the score go down approximately 100 points.

When you file a bankruptcy, you can start rebuilding your credit score just as soon as you are discharged from your debts. If you file a Chapter 7, you will receive your discharge about 90 days after filing. A Chapter 13 discharge is usually not received until you've completed your three to five-year payment plan. So if you have a choice of what kind of bankruptcy to file, you might consider choosing Chapter 7 so that you receive a discharge sooner and can start rebuilding. Your attorney will give you more information so you can decide which filing is best for your situation.

When you receive a bankruptcy discharge, new potential creditors know that old creditors cannot get judgments against you or interrupt your income flow by garnishing wages. Thus you will be more able to pay their debt. They also know you can't file bankruptcy again and get any kind of discharge (Chapter 7 or 13) for at least four years, making it even more likely that they will be able to collect from you. So your score will go up. Future creditors will like you better.

The trick is - how do you rebuild your credit score after bankruptcy? More important, how does one create a mindset that supports successful financial transformation? To support the process of transformation and make it easier to remember, I've put together an acronym: **PHOENIX**.

P is for Plan. Map out the steps you are going to take to recreate a positive credit picture. For instance, your plan should include:

1. Write down everything you spend for a month. Figure out where your money is going. Then look at where you can economize. Can you modify or refinance your mortgage to a lower payment? Can you refinance your car for a lower payment? Compare five different companies for auto insurance and choose the lowest company. You will find that prices vary widely. But make sure you don't give up important coverages such as comprehensive and collision insurance and underinsured motorist coverage.

2. Collect and bank $1000 cash. You might do this by selling things you have that no longer serve you. Garage sales aren't necessarily the highest dollar way to sell things. Think about Craig's List or EBay instead.

3. Get a secured credit card by putting the cash in a savings account and then asking the bank or credit union for a secured credit card. Only charge up to 30% of the limit and pay it off completely each month. Your credit score will be higher if you don't borrow more than 30% of your credit line. And if you pay it off in full, then you don't pay any interest! The savings account

also helps future creditors trust your future credit worthiness.

4. Start a savings plan where you save something from each pay check. Experts recommend saving 10% to 20% of each pay check. But if you don't think you can go that high, save 5%. I promise you won't notice it missing from your paycheck. And when you need tires or a car repair, you won't need to touch the credit card because you will have the money in savings.

5. Don't buy things on credit. If you need furniture, save money and buy something you can afford or buy something used. If your car is broken, fix it rather than buying a new one. If you must replace it, buy something used that you by for cash. Use your resources. Be creative. For instance, one of my clients fixes up found furniture and sells it for money. By found, I mean found by the side of the road. She's very creative. There are many ways you can be creative, too!

6. Increase your income if you need to. Look at part time jobs or services you can render to others that they will pay for. I recommend that you look at Loral Langmeier's book *The Millionaire Maker's Guide to Creating a Cash Machine for Life*. She describes a process where anyone can create a side business using strengths and skills they already have.

H is for Honesty. Be honest with yourself. Look at the actions you take regarding money, your spending habits. I find that having an accountability partner – someone I share my goals and dreams with – keeps me honest. So if I tell my accountability partner that my goal is to save 10% of every paycheck in my retirement plan, she will ask me how that's going. Having a partner serves two purposes: 1) I follow through with my plan because I want to make sure she believes I'm strong, and 2) my partner won't put up with my excuses for why I didn't do what I said I would do. She'll call me on my stuff. If you are married or in partnership with someone, ask your partner to join you in an accountability partnership. Otherwise choose a friend who shares similar goals.

O is for being Open to new ideas, new ways of doing things. After all, your best thinking got you where you were – in bankruptcy. In my own commitment to rising from the ashes (after all I must practice what I preach) I have to admit that how I managed my finances in the past did not create the financial future and flexibility to visit my grandchildren in Colorado as I want to. I'm constantly researching and sharing with others new ways of doing things.

E - Examine your financial habits. Ask yourself, do I shop impulsively? Impulse shopping is not very conducive to having a successful financial plan. Do you find yourself saying, "I can't afford that" when you need or want something? If it's something really important, reframe that into, "How can I manage that?" Then think creatively.

N - Never, never, never, never give up! If you don't do well one day, start over again the next day. Call your friend or accountability partner and get some encouragement. Shake it off, then keep on working your plan, refining your plan and realize the success that is yours by right.

I – Imagine. Take at least 10 minutes every day to imagine your life when you have built financial stability and realized your dream. Focus on an actual date in your mind for the dream to come true. If you want a house of your own, imagine what the house is like. Walk in the front door in your mind and look around and appreciate the space that is your own. Imagine your family enjoying the home. If you want a place you can entertain, imagine your first holiday dinner in the home.

X - Expect to improve your financial situation and your credit score. Expect the Best. If you are taking steps to improve your financial situation, but you don't really expect that it will work, your spectacular results may not happen; they'll be inconsistent at best.

I'd love you to go ahead and join me in my **Being the Phoenix** project. My website, www.BeThePhoenix.net contains blog posts, news about upcoming publications, an archive of Ask the Expert tele classes, webinars and many more dynamic tools to help you rise from the ashes. Here's to your financial rebirth today!

If you are interested in speaking with me, you may contact me at KathrynHathaway@BeThePhoenix.net. I would love to continue the conversation with you. Rise, my friends, rise!

ABOUT THE AUTHOR

Kathryn A. Hathaway, the Founder of Being The Phoenix, LLC, provides resources and support for rising from the ashes of financial ruin to claim the abundant life you're meant to live. For more information visit the website at www.BeThePhoenix.net.

She is a practicing attorney at Hathaway Sprague Law, P.A. in Northern Florida and a board certified expert in consumer bankruptcy law. With more than 29 years of legal experience, including bankruptcy, probate, asset protection and estate planning, she is 100% committed to helping individuals rebuild their lives despite financial challenges and set backs. She is dedicated to meeting the legal needs of her clients when their most important financial matters are at stake.

Kathryn looks not just to the situation at hand, but also assists clients in visualizing a better future on the other side of the current legal problem. She is a Certified Professional Speaker and has addressed a wide variety of audiences on topics from bankruptcy, the interplay between divorce and bankruptcy law, estate planning, as well as on inspirational/spiritual subjects. Her law firm website is www.HathawayLaw.net.

CHAPTER **10**

GIVE YOURSELF MORE CREDIT THAN THAT

Beth Johnston

I always thought credit scores ranked among such topics as age and weight; topics "ladies" just don't talk about. You always knew "it was there", you just did your best to avoid it. The less said, the better. It was when I had the great pleasure of meeting Patricia Giankas that my total lack of understanding about credit score became embarrassingly evident to me. I previously believed one's credit score was 100% the result of buying behaviors and making on-time minimum payments, thereby keeping negative reports at arm's length. Reasonable, right?

After a one-hour conversation with Patricia, my entire perspective changed. By putting Patricia's tips to work for myself, I increased my credit score by 60 point in about 5 months! It was easy, it took no time, and the results speak for themselves! Patricia enlightened me and empowered me all at the same time and I want to share some of the basic principles that this grateful student learned...

Making minimum monthly payments doesn't get the job done (it also makes everything more expensive!). Patricia taught me that actually making larger payments ahead of schedule is a much better approach – and she was right. Amazingly, lack of positive activity on a credit score report often does less good than negative activity. This seemed counter-intuitive at first, but by creating more positive activity, my credit score began to go up immediately. By making a series of small purchases followed by a series of small payments, positive activity on my report increased. Fascinating!

Carrying a wallet-full of credit cards can seem somewhat exciting but is definitely not necessary. Having even just one major credit card that you manage properly can serve your credit score better than many small accounts. Also, many banks are offering enticing promotions for cash-back or rewards points programs that pay you as you pay them.

We've all heard the term "timing is everything", so it goes with credit, as well. When you apply for a loan may not be as arbitrary as you think. The actual day you apply for a mortgage, a car loan, a business loan, etc. can make all the difference in whether you get it, or not. Who knew? When I purchased a new car in 2015, I was able to finance the entire cost. My previous attempt required 25% down. Fabulous!

In today's world, more households are headed by women, more new businesses are started by women, and women often out-earn their male counterparts (despite the 76% earning-deficit issue!). Women need to be well-informed about credit score, how they work and how much easier it really is to manage.

Knowing that I can have more control over my credit score has given me a sense of greater control over my life. I am not a victim of a system that controls me, I am a predictor of a system I can truly be in greater control of. I can control it; I no longer allow it to control me. In putting these simple tips to work for myself, I was able to refinance my home mortgage. The lower rate will shave me tens of thousands of dollars over the life of the loan. PLUS, I knew exactly WHEN to apply for it!

I imagine we have all heard overwhelmingly uncomfortable stories of debt consuming relationships, happiness, even health. How wonderful to think such outcomes can be avoided by having better information, greater understanding, and a more proactive approach to credit.

Managing my credit has become a bit of a game; a fun game with great reward for doing a better job. Sixty points in 5-months has served me well and I cannot appreciate Patricia Giankas more for sharing her amazing knowledge and truly simplifying what I imagined was beyond my ability to control. As in all cases, information is powerful. Putting information to work for yourself is empowering. Taking control of your credit score is an action-reaction, input equals output scenario that becomes fun to manage and satisfying when experiencing the results.

May I encourage you to learn more about your credit score and how you can take greater control of your financial future and the security of your family? I hope so.

Go ahead...give yourself more credit!

ABOUT THE AUTHOR

Beth Johnston is an entrepreneur of the truest kind. Beth is a published author, coach, consultant, mentor and managing editor of Inspirational Woman magazine. She combines creative thinking with mathematical skills as a graduate-level and business-events speaker.

The oldest daughter in a large family, Beth says she was born in to management and learned good listening skills sitting around the dining room table.

Beth believes need and opportunity are the winning combination, co-operation trumps competition and collaborative relationships are not only smart, but economically efficient and effective.

As the the Founder of The International Women's Leadership Association (TheIWLA) Beth currently serves as its Executive Director and continues to do motivational coaching.

Learn more about TheIWLA at www.TheIWLA.com or connect with Beth at beth@theiwla.com.

CHAPTER 11

FISCAL FITNESS
BUILDING YOUR NEST INVESTMENT

Karen Mayfield

My earliest memory of working for money was when I was around 5 years old. My Father's family were row croppers who grew soybeans and cotton. I learned to pick cotton at an early age; and at that early stage of my life I remember receiving money from the sale of my bags full of cotton. As I grew up, I worked at cleaning houses for different people and made even more money.

I was fifteen when I first experienced entrepreneurism. I was lured into my now current career choice of entrepreneurism by a tabloid magazine ad I was reading in line at the grocery store checkout one day. I bought the magazine, took it home and sent off for my very first "work-at-home getting paid to stuff envelopes get rich quick scheme." For only $49.95 I could get set up in my own business. That is a small amount in today's world as an investment to get started in business but in 1970 that was a lot of money and it took every bit of the money I had saved from picking cotton or cleaning houses to get started.

I'll always remember the excitement I had the day I came home from school and saw all the boxes on the front porch. I rushed inside, throwing all my stuff down and rushed back outside to bring in the workings of my first million-dollar opportunity. Fast-forward about 500 envelopes and my get-rich-quick scheme was losing its luster. I had lured my great grand-mother and my grand-mother into my enterprising operation. Then, somewhere around 1,000 envelopes they both up and quit. Without notice mind you...

Now as a solo-preneur I was left with getting another 8500 envelopes stuffed, by myself just to make $100 and part of that money I owed to my previous employees; my grandmas. While I was complaining that my first get rich quick adventure was not such a good idea after all, my grand-mother freely shares her wisdom with me when she made the statement:

> *"Ideas are a dime a dozen and without a dozen people on one idea it will never be worth a dime".*

To which, at that time, I rolled my eyes. Today I recognize those words as great wisdom. After a lot of work I finally got all 10,000 envelopes stuffed, delivered to the post-office and sent off. I awaited my riches, the payment from my efforts, to be delivered in the mail. Five days later, I received my $100 check. Woo Hoo! I paid off my grand-mothers earned wages of $18.00, made back my original $49.95 investment and had a profit of $32. Yee Haa!

I decided that with the practice of the first run of envelopes, I now had a system and I decided to roll the dice and order another 10,000 envelopes for $49.95. This time, I hired no employees, stuffed the envelopes in record time, delivered to the post office and started the process all over again. I repeated the process over and over again until I was out of high school. It took a while, but eventually I was working out of my profit and not my pocket.

Then it happened....I broke my little finger and was unable to stuff envelopes. Just that fast, I was out of business.

Entrepreneurism is one of the fastest growing endeavors in the world of careerism today. The risk and rewards are both high. You can be soaring with the eagles, getting a birds-eye view of the best life has to offer one minute and just as easily be grounded the next. In order to succeed, you must have the Fiscal Fitness to withstand the slings and arrows of outrageous fortune and the doom and gloom of Fiscal Failure. It's time to be fiscally prepared to flex your financial muscles!

Just like any other fitness program Fiscal Fitness is much the same. There are certain things you will need in your Fitness bag:

1. A GOOD CREDIT SCORE.

A low credit score will cost you in higher interest rates. This makes your payments higher and you spend a lot more in interest getting your debt paid off. High interest rates are not in your "nest interest".

2. A WORKOUT SHEET (WHERE DO YOU SPEND YOUR MONEY?)

Start tracking where you spend your money and look for your *Fiscal Fitness* weak spots. Remember this is a fitness program; if you were in the physical fitness program, I'm sure you would want to work up to the heavier weights. Credit is much the same. When you are first starting a *Fiscal Fitness* program, it's best to start small and build from there. Being loaded down with debt is not great for you physically or fiscally.

3. CREDIT REPAIR OR RESTORATION PROGRAM.

Let's face it, life happens. You're soaring with the eagles one minute, then you are down and out with the injured turkeys the next. My friend's husband was a professional athlete. During the time he was playing his sport, he injured his knee and was benched for a couple of seasons. He then played for one season and was injured again; this time he was forced to retire. Their income ceased immediately, his job was gone and his career as an athlete was over. For most people, this is life altering and overwhelming news. It could be the end of someone's *Fiscal Fitness*. But my friends' lives continued, must less effected by the trauma of his losing his job than most, because they had established great credit, great retirement planning and had saved and invested wisely in planning for life after athletics. They practiced great *Fiscal Fitness*.

Another friend is a very successful business person in her own right. She is an entrepreneur and very successful in her career. One day she was involved in a three car accident and was out of work for over 18 months. Her credit was finished, she had no savings, as she had always lived in the moment and mindset of "I want what I want when I want it", and never planned for the rainy season (that would eventually come), when the sun was shining brightly. Basically, she had NO *Fiscal Fitness* plan. After finding rock bottom, the climb back to credit worthiness and fiscal stability finally became possible after five years.

4. FIND A FITNESS BUDDY (SOMEONE TO HOLD YOU ACCOUNTABLE).

This could be a spouse, a friend, a business partner or even an online Fiscal buddy who is equally invested in their own *Fiscal Fitness* program and can use your support. This will give you the support you will need when you are on the verge of giving up or slipping in your fitness program. Sometimes just that little extra support makes a big difference.

5. GATHER ANY INFORMATION THAT OFFERS SOUND FISCAL ADVICE AND IMPLEMENT WHAT SUITS YOUR FISCAL NEEDS.

In my *Fiscal Fitness* bag, I have designed a 33-33-33 program. My fixed expenses must be only 33% of my net income, 33% is for savings and investments, 33% is divided equally three ways for spending, giving away, and emergency fund and 1% goes into a discretionary fund. This has worked well for me and if you can't come up with a fiscal system to help you budget on your own, feel free to contact me online for a quick consultation at: Karen@wakeupwomen.com. *Dave Ramsey's Financial Peace University* is another great way to turn finances around. There are great free tools available online at various websites from many well-known financial experts. Just ask Google!

Here's the deal...It is not in your "nest interest" to pay high interest rates to have credit. The "nest egg" you were planning to have later in life will potentially fall out of your "nest" with a few little miscalculations. Keep a great credit score. If you encounter a glitch in your plan and fiscally things change, a good plan to get you back on track ASAP is necessary. Be open to support, search for social media groups who have the same situation as you, and participate in restoration conversation there. There are lots of people out there in the same boat!

And as my grandmother shared with me years ago:

> *"If your outgo exceeds to your income your upkeep will be your downfall"*

Create a great Fiscal Fitness program and fill your nest egg with Golden Nuggets...

ABOUT THE AUTHOR

Karen Mayfield, Msc…CCC
Karen is a CTA certified coach, Metaphysical Minister, creator of the Posivity Factor Life Success Plan. She is also co-creator, author and publisher in the best-selling Wake up Women and Conversations that Make a Difference book series.

Karen is a former Mars Venus facilitator. Her twenty years of experience in print advertising, ad copy, and print media campaigns, combined with her fifteen years in training mid to upper management provides Karen with the background in niche marketing needed in today's spiritually emerging market and economy.

Karen is co-creator of Wake Up Women, which ultimately allows people the experience of Peace of Mind as a state of mind.

Utilizing the Laws of Attraction in thought, clarity and action, Karen now lives a life she loves. Being a mom, grandmother, friend, and member in a family of entrepreneurial women is the inspiration behind Karen's purpose. "When you wake up a woman, she will wake up the world around her." Life experiences have provided Karen with the wisdom needed to assist others in living a life they love.

Connect with Karen at Karen@wakeupwomen.com.

CHAPTER 12

TAKING A LEAP OF FAITH
MONEY, DREAMS & SHOW BIZ

Barbara Niven

I am still pinching myself that I've been living my dream of being an Actress for over half my life now. I am living proof that no matter how crazy your dream or goal may be; you can find a way to achieve it. It starts with choosing to take a leap of faith.

At the beginning all I had was a dream, and there were huge odds stacked against me. I was almost 30 years old, a newly-divorced single mother of a four-year-old, living in Portland, Oregon. I had no knowledge of the acting biz, and no role models to turn to. Money was scarce and scary because I didn't receive child support. I'd been a stay-at-home mom who didn't graduate college, so my job skills weren't exactly marketable. But

I knew in my heart that I was here for a purpose. I knew I was supposed to be an actress who made a difference in the world through my work.

My daughter was counting on me, so I took stock of my skills. I was a camera ham, and I loved to write. So I thought, "I bet I could be a TV reporter." In my case, ignorance was bliss. I didn't know enough about it to know what hurdles I'd have to leap over.

The next day I showed up at the door of the News Director at the NBC affiliate in Portland and said, "Will you please mentor me? If I bring you stories, will you give me feedback so I can get better? Because I am telling you right now that I am going to work for you!" He was taken aback but liked my moxie, so he said yes. I brought him story after story, and he helped me sharpen my skills. Finally, he put me on as an intern (an unpaid position) and, against all odds, I sold my first story to NBC network!

Turns out I liked reporting, but I didn't love it. That old acting bug kept haunting me. So I went to a book store and bought a book on acting. That book changed my life and opened up a whole new world. I was hooked, and determined to find a way to make it happen!

At this point my bank account was zilch, and despite some help from Mom and Dad, I had to use my credit card more than I wanted. I considered it a calculated risk, an investment in myself and my future. I prayed that I would soon get enough traction to start paying off my debts. Believe me, there were a lot of sleepless nights before that would eventually happen.

I dove into acting full speed ahead. I found an acting class, got an agent and took headshots. I learned that besides TV and Film roles, there are other ways to make money in show business. Bread and butter jobs for actors include TV and radio commercials, industrial films, being a spokesperson, doing voice-overs, presenting at trade shows, hosting talk shows, pitching infomercials, etc. I did it all! I even became a top fitness model for companies like NIKE.

Every day I would knock on doors or make phone calls to drum up business, asking someone at an ad agency or a production company if they could use me for a project. I created relationships, and before long I became the "go to" girl in the Pacific Northwest for all those categories. People hired me over and over again because they could count on me to give a good performance. But even more importantly, I brought joy and good energy to the set.

That's one of my secrets. People hire people they like to be around. I always tell newbie actors that creating relationships is key. Getting booked for a job is great, but it's only ONE job. Repeat business is what will give you a career. That holds true for any industry.

Finally, I was making good money and was out of debt. I was working non-stop, but I wasn't doing theatrical acting (Film or TV), which is the reason I'd gone into the business in the first place. I had reached a plateau of possibilities in my hometown of Portland, and to go any farther I needed to move to Hollywood. It was scary, because I'd have to leave my support system and start over!

I thought about it long and hard. I hesitated to uproot my daughter and change her life simply to follow my dream. Plus, it was a gamble. The competition is much stiffer in Hollywood, especially for a new actress. Acting roles and the money they bring usually don't come in that fast. But I was lucky. I booked a job as a game show host for MGM/UA as soon as I got there (thank you, "Straight to the Heart!") and soon got auditions that turned into screen tests (thank you, ABC!), and I started booking roles in TV and films.

It still wasn't enough to support us steadily though. As an actress, you never know when the next job will come in, and there can be long dry spells. Plus, I had to spend a lot on classes, headshots, demo reels, casting director workshops, etc. I had to be so careful with my money, and sometimes there wasn't enough to go around.

To make dollars stretch, my daughter Jess and I lived with roommates and we shared a bed. I couldn't afford to buy her school lunches, so I packed her lunch every day (with a love note written on her napkin). Our big treat was to go to Taco Bell, because we could both eat everything we wanted for less than $5! During the Christmas season, we kept the table full of craft materials and had fun making homemade presents.

One Christmas Eve I'll never forget. Jess and I saw a homeless man and his old dog shivering outside a supermarket. He had taken off his own jacket to wrap around his beloved pet. It was heart-breaking. We went inside the store and giggled as we loaded up our shopping cart with dog food, blankets and other gifts. Outside, as Jess proudly offered it to him, she said "Merry Christmas". It was an incredible feeling to be able to give to someone who had less than we did, and I was proud of my daughter for being so selfless. It was our best Christmas ever.

What's funny is that when we look back on those struggling days, we both say it was probably the richest time of our lives. We formed an incredible bond that continues today. By sharing that journey with me, she not only learned the value of money, but also the importance of following one's heart.

At that time in my life, even though I was trying to be so careful, I did get into credit card trouble. We had several emergencies that added up. A huge vet bill. A trip to the emergency room. A dental crown. I had no options except to use my credit card and pray I would get a job so I could pay it off quickly. To this day, I still quake at opening a bill from a credit card company or a creditor because I remember what it felt like to not be able to pay them. I did learn a big lesson about creditors though. They want to work with you. Being pro-active and communicating with them like a real person instead of burying your head in the sand is key. For instance, when I had a dental emergency, I asked the dentist if I could pay it off $25 a month and he said yes! I was so proud to pay that last bill, knowing that I had kept my ethics and my honor in place.

It's vital to be ethical and trustworthy in money matters. That's what having good credit means, that people can trust you. Once you've lost that trust it can take a lot of time and work to get it back, and in today's internet age there's no hiding.

Good credit gives you freedom, self-confidence, and the luxury of choice. You can use it at your discretion to take calculated steps toward achieving goals, no matter what they may be. Maybe it's to purchase a car, have a baby, buy a home, start a business, go back to school, take a dream vacation, or help out friends and family members. With a stellar credit rating, you will be ready for anything!

Having great credit is one of my proudest accomplishments. It's allowed me to purchase a house I love, start my Unleash Your Star Power!™ business, open a video studio, offer support to my daughter when she was on bed rest during her pregnancy, assist a friend when she lost her job, and so much more. But the best part is that it gives me a feeling of security I wouldn't trade for the world.

I wish I'd learned this at a much earlier age. I never learned any kind of finance skills in school, and it still makes me mad. It would have saved me so much stress. I had to learn the hard way, and then dig myself out of situations that could have been prevented.

Why don't we teach our kids the basics of how to open a bank account, balance a checkbook, the importance of putting money into savings each month, the how-tos of applying for and using a credit card, the pros and cons of using said credit card, how to pay bills, how to keep an organized "paper flow" in the household, how to do taxes, what a pension is, how to plan for retirement, etc.? When you're young, none of these things seem to matter much. But you wise up pretty quickly when you get older and you are buried in piles of paper, unpaid bills and bad credit. I am speaking from experience.

Today, even though I currently have a good income from acting, I try to spend money wisely. I think it's because I remember what it was like to be in money panic, and the feeling of being safe and secure now outweighs the adrenalin rush of buying things. I honestly don't need that much though. For me, simple is better. I am not a clothes shopper. I do my own manicures and pedicures. I proudly drive a 2005 Prius with 65,000 miles on it. I cook my meals and rarely go out to restaurants, not only because I eat healthier that way, but it saves money. Even when I'm traveling on location I try to always stay in a place with a kitchen so I can shop for groceries and cook there too. It keeps me grounded and on a diet. (When you're an actress, that's important because the camera really does add ten pounds. Sigh.)

I do spend money on my home environment and the people (and animals) I love. I spoil my grandchildren like crazy, but it's not about buying them "things". I spend a lot of time with them, and if I do buy them gifts, it's something that's interactive, that we can do as a family.

Last year I took another huge leap of faith financially. I sold my condo and bought a house. It's not a Beverly Hills mansion by any means, but I am thrilled with it! I have been adding personal touches to make it my own and will remodel bit by bit as I earn more in the future. But I won't get ahead of myself. Acting is never a steady job, and a TV series can get canceled at any time.

Have good credit gave me options when I was house-hunting. I was able to get a great interest rate because of it. I had also saved enough to pay my mortgage down to the point where I have a low monthly payment that I will always be able to afford, no matter what happens in my career. I can't tell you what peace of mind that brings.

Being smart with money is a mindset. No matter how much you are making, my advice is to never live above your means. Instead, savor the little things and show your children by example that it's more important to feel secure and happy than it is to have the latest car, or a big house that you have to stretch to get into and then worry about keeping. Choosing to live beneath your means lets you sleep at night. It also allows you to stockpile a nest egg, and a nest egg gives you options.

I have a few other tips that have worked for me too. One is to get a good accountant and/or financial advisor. You don't have to wait until you're "rich" to do it, because no matter what stage you're at they'll probably point out ways for you to save more money than you could ever do without them, so they'll basically pay for themselves. Another is to get organized with your paper flow and streamline your financial processes. Finally, listen to and hire experts in areas you are not an expert in.

I am never going to be great at finances and numbers. It's just not my thing, and I'd rather spend my time being creative (which brings in income) instead of getting bogged down in those kinds of details. So one of the best things I ever did was to hire an accountant, someone who is good at all the things I am not. I incorporated several years ago, and the rules and regulations are confusing to me! Not complying perfectly can not only be expensive, it can mess up your credit score and/or line of credit. The money I pay my dear accountant is some of the best money I have ever spent! They know better than I ever could exactly what I can write off on my corporate and personal income. Plus, they file all the government forms, give me sound financial advice, and prepare my taxes. All I have to do is sign on the dotted line. A word of caution here though. If you hire someone to do this, make sure they are reputable and trustworthy, because they will have access to your finances. Stay in control and on top of it!

I live by the motto, "Be calm and simple in your life, so you can be powerful and original in your work." To me, being organized is key. If you're buried in piles of paperwork, why not give yourself the gift of decluttering your life? An easy way to get organized is to buy a filing cabinet with manila folders. I ordered one online and had it delivered the next day. It's so satisfying to create structure out of chaos!

I keep every single receipt (so I have a record of everything I spend money on) and file them into monthly folders. When I'm traveling I put receipts in a Ziploc bag and label it with the dates and client I'm working for. When I get home I pop them into the monthly file. At the end of the year, all the files and paperwork go into a box for tax purposes. Organizing yourself this way not only gets rid of overwhelm and "paper chaos", you can also find things easily when you need a receipt or a phone number.

I've also streamlined my financial processes. Online banking has been my lifesaver, especially because I travel so much. I can quickly sign on to my account from wherever I am in the world, check my balances, and pay a bill. I have most of my bills on auto-pay, so I don't have to worry that something will fall through the cracks and affect my credit. I have set up daily banking alerts for each of my accounts so I know exactly where I stand every morning by email. I also get notifications about my American Express card. I have an app on my iPhone that texts me immediately whenever a charge goes through. I can track activity and payments and see my statement right on my phone. I love modern technology!

We can't be good at everything, so I listen to experts and follow their coaching. For instance, I heard Suze Orman say we must always keep six months of a financial cushion put aside in case of emergency. I try my best to adhere to that. She's a smart woman, because keeping your finances in order allows you to take risks. When you have a cushion, you can take calculated leaps of faith toward your dreams!

I have achieved success in many things in my life only because I chose to take those leaps of faith. Now when something scares me, I know I have to do it! I call it "following my goose bumps". I have found that my biggest fear almost always turns out to be my biggest gold, and the "fear" is really just excitement and anticipation. I've seen that in my media training clients too. The ones who are most afraid of the camera or of public speaking usually turn out to be the best at it!

Life should not be spent working 24/7 chasing a paycheck. Where's the joy in that? Instead, find something you absolutely love to do, something that gives you goose bumps, and figure out how to incorporate it into your life. Even if you don't earn money from it, your spirit will soar and you will be richer than you can imagine. You will wake up every day with passion, excited to be living your dream.

That sums up my life as an actress. It's not rational. It's not safe. There's no security in it. In fact, I have lived on way too much Top Ramen at times. But I wouldn't trade it for the world. I look back at the beginning oh so many years ago and remember thinking, "I don't want to wonder **WHAT IF** at the end of my life. I have to at least TRY." 30 years later that still holds true and it still drives me. I refuse to sit back and "settle". Instead I am always looking to expand, to learn new things, to create my next project, to make a bigger difference. To experience goose bumps.

That initial huge leap of faith changed the course of my life. That's my wish for you too. If you have a dream, you owe it to yourself to try. You only have one life, and it is short. Don't spend time wishing it away. Instead, leap into it! I've leaped out of my comfort zone so many times. But only when you get out of your comfort zone can you see how high you can fly!

"Live your passion. Connect to your purpose. Make a difference. And... don't give up five minutes before the miracle!"

ABOUT THE AUTHOR

Award-winning actress Barbara Niven currently stars in the prime time TV series' "Chesapeake Shores" & "Murder She Baked" for Hallmark Channel, NBC's Emmy Award-winning "Parks and Recreation", "Hamlet's Ghost" which premiered at the Cannes Film Festival, and the independent comedy-horror feature "Suburban Gothic".

In addition to the 100+ Film and TV credits to her name, Barbara has gained international acclaim as Hollywood's Top Media Trainer and Video Marketing Coach. She created Unleash Your Star Power! to help others hone their message, makeover their professional image, handle nerves, and use video to dominate their niche. She works with new and established business owners, professionals, CEOs, entrepreneurs, hosts, speakers and authors from her studio in Los Angeles where she offers custom video production services, one-on-one coaching and her popular Video Boot Camps. Her new online academy is premiering soon.

She is also a Celebrity Motivational Speaker and best-selling author. Business and Motivational topics include *Unleash Your Star Power!, Be a Video Marketing Superstar, ACT as IF and Eating Disorders & Pressures to Be Perfect*. For more information, visit www.UnleashYourStarPower.com.

CHAPTER **13**

WEALTHY MIND EQUALS WEALTHY WALLET

Yvonne Oswald PhD

Master your words and you shape your life. Master your thoughts and you shape your destiny! Your mind is your GPS of life.

Why is it that some people have the ability to make and keep money easily and others aren't able to manage, even though they may have the same amount of education and competence? There are only three things that make the biggest difference to financial accomplishment: healthy self-esteem, the ability to model effective success, and the ability to be adaptable and flexible. All of these aspects are controlled by a healthy mind. Success, quite simply, is a formula. So how do you go about getting these amazing and easily achievable skill sets?

The first and most important thing to do is to set your GPS correctly. Your Global Positioning System for your life needs to be accurately predetermined if you are to reach your final destination of comfort, enjoyment and freedom. The ultimate purpose in life is to fulfil your destiny; the job you were sent here to do. And a strong mind equals a strong and powerful destiny.

It seems that logic and reasoning are obviously involved when we are thinking about getting more money. However, there is one thing that is often overlooked. The most important thing you'll ever do to increase your credit in the bank and in life is to focus on working on your self-esteem. Loving yourself is essential to increasing wealth. What manifests in your life mirrors what you believe you are and have inside yourself. The amount of money you attract indirectly correlates to the amount you believe you are worthy of receiving, therefore the more you believe in yourself, the more your potential financial worth will increase.

Your self-image directs your GPS to your destiny.

Your self-esteem is your most prized possession. You bring the unique talents you were born with to the world and you don't have the luxury of not sharing them. We need you to come up and offer them like a gift at the altar so that we can learn from them. It will also bring to you magical moments when you remember who you are...who you really are. Once you get in tune with that, then you have acceptance, inner peace, harmony and understanding; which give you direct access to freedom and abundance on every level.

So how do you go about feeling good about yourself? You begin by changing the way you speak to yourself. You create your world with your words; your self-talk actually produces 100% of all the results in your life. Your mind only processes the keywords you use; it works exactly like the Internet. Grammar and context have little value to the mind, as it needs to respond instantly, so it focuses on intent and keywords. A good way to begin changing your mind to focus on the positive is to get a Switch Buddy, as I suggest in my book, Every Word has Power, and ask them to switch your language. Every time you say something like, "Don't worry," your switch buddy will say "Switch!" and you can replace it with "You'll be fine." In just two weeks you'll be amazed at how quickly you think and act more positively.

Secondly, reward yourself daily (a good book, a nice tea, a show, a hobby, a fun night out) and focus daily on what is working in your life by having a gratitude book by your bed to write three things that you are grateful for at the end of every day. And believe me I know that some days you are going to write: I breathed today. I'm still here. Tomorrow is almost here. Thank God!

When you focus on what is not you, or what you don't have, you focus only on the clouds above your head that stop the sunlight from streaming in. That is like focusing on a shadow and thinking it real. Focus clearly on where you have set your GPS and you will always be above the clouds, basking in the light of the sun, where everything is possible, nourishing your soul. Remember that a powerful oak tree grows from a small acorn by simply absorbing sunlight and water.

A nun came to see me for a three-hour breakthrough session and we were working on aligning her values.

She had been questioning her faith and wondering why she was feeling separated from her calling. She insisted that her top value was being humble and unworthy. I thought for a while and then asked her if God is humble or unworthy. "Oh, no! God is great and glorious. Humbleness and unworthiness is not a part of God. "Hmm," I said, "Then it is not so fortunate that you are not part of God, isn't it?" When she asked me to explain I told her that since she was humble, and humbleness is not a part of God, then she must remain separate from God as long as she remained humble and unworthy. She looked confused and then said, "Take those off the list! Put at the top: God, love and light! I am full of light and glory and oneness. That's amazing! I actually feel wonderful and close to God just saying that!" She left smiling and full of confidence and enthusiasm again. So let us go ahead and align you with your highest purpose to direct the intent for your success.

At its most elemental level, money is energy, or manna, which the Merriam-Webster dictionary defines as "spiritual nourishment of divine origin." In nature, a powerful river starts out as a trickle, then turns into a brook, then a stream, then into a watercourse and then into a rushing river speeding to the open sea as it gathers momentum. As you open your mind to greater possibilities and higher purpose, your money energy also begins to flow more swiftly. So when you decide to make more money, the most important question to ask your self is WHY? For what purpose do you want more money? Is it to just get out of debt, which will only lead you to more debt, or can you turn your head in a different direction and ask yourself ; "What is most important to me in life?" What is the bigger question that will set your goals to a higher intent? Is it to leave a legacy? Is it so that you can enjoy life? Is it so that your children can have more than you had? Is it for fame or recognition? Is it for fulfilment? Let's begin by finding what you regard as significant in life.

WHAT IS REALLY IMPORTANT TO YOU?

Answer these questions quickly please:

1. What or who do you value most in life?
2. Whose work do you admire the most (famous person)? What is it about them that you admire? Can you model them? How did they begin? Go to their website and model it. They spent thousands of dollars on marketing and you can easily make yours similar.
3. What positive advice would you give the 16-year-old you if you could talk to her/him right now? What could you say to encourage her/him? "You don't know it yet, but you will have…You will be …You will do amazing things. You will…"
4. What do you want people to say about you at your eulogy? What will they say you did to make a difference?
5. When your grandchildren or your friends' children tell stories about you what is the one thing you want them to remember about you?
6. How many people have you had a positive influence on? Who in particular are you proud to have helped?
7. What are you an expert in being, doing or getting? Can you find someone who has those same talents who is making money by using them and model them? Or can you find someone who has

a talent for making money and become an expert like them by studying the same subject?

8. What phrase or phrases sums up life for you?

The reason you need to ask yourself these questions is that your answers reflect what is fundamental to your happiness; these qualities act as your touch points and are to be brought in as your guidelines for life. The questions will also set your mind on a search for resources to bring you greater opportunities. All change and all learning is unconscious (although the decision to change is made by the conscious mind), so it is by sending your mind on a fresh and interesting quest to expand your imagination that you will get new results in your life. If your imagination and willpower had a competition, your imagination (the tool of the unconscious) would win every time. In fact, if it were up to willpower (the conscious mind's tool) we'd have all been successful long ago!

The human mind is the most powerful device available to mankind. Your unconscious mind is a servo mechanism. That means it is like a magic genie in a lamp that simply requires you to tell it what to do and it is mandated to follow the suggestion literally, unless there is a threat (or a perceived threat) to health, in which case it will over-ride conscious directions. It is programmed to constantly adapt and grow. The compelling force of your inner mind is with you when directed consistently. It handles more than 2,000,000 bits of information every second, so making you rich is easy for it, as long as you learn to direct it properly and trust it completely.

You were born with DNA inherited from two parents, along with DNA survival information gathered and formulated by generations of people through millenniums.

The extent to which different genes become activated or turned off is significantly influenced by your childhood environment and experiences, as well as your emotions and the early training you received, that deep wires your neural pathways.

The great news is that the recently discovered neuroplasticity of the brain means that we can influence gene structure to bring about dynamic change in our gene expression, while simultaneously promoting growth of new neural pathways; that means that we can simply delete old files and install new ones. The brain, which is the interface between the mind and body, can actually be engineered to change and transform old non supportive beliefs into new, supportive beliefs and behaviors. Mind directing has been proven to increase the synchronicity of the two-way communication between the brain and the body, restoring coherence. The corresponding feelings of comfortable wellbeing lead to confident actions, producing powerful, successful results.

Influencing the mind is easy once you realize that it requires a direct command and repetition to make it respond, rather than a vague wish or a hope. When you learn to issue a command rather than a hope, you are in charge of the biggest search engine and the most effective results bringer on the planet. Act as if you have it now and be authoritative in asking for your needs to be met. Order your mind to obey and it has to follow your summons; especially with repeated instructions. A daily mantra such as, "Money constantly flows into my life like a waterfall." increases your chance of success. Set your goal, repeat, repeat, repeat and then let it go and get on with having fun in your life. It is important to detach from the result after you have set the events in motion. Thinking too much about what you want is like trying to remember the name of someone that is on the tip of your tongue. The more you try the more it slips on by.

How do you detach? When my daughter Katherine completed her performing arts degree she started going for auditions. After every audition she would ask herself – "What exactly just happened in the room? Did I do well? What could I have done better?" She was disappointed if she didn't get a call back and then would analyze and think the audition through all over again. Upon finding out how she had been dealing with auditions, one of her professors gave her some fabulous advice; he said to her, "Train, learn, rehearse and do your best. Go for the audition, show them the best of what you have, leave the room and let it go. If you are what they want, you'll get a call back. If not, then keep going until you get the next audition. Once it's done, it's done. Move on." She has now taken this advice to heart and she has done amazingly well since she started to apply it. Sound advice for life on a daily basis! After you have sent out your thoughts and wishes and goals, move on and release them so that God can decide which part in his next play to offer you.

PRACTICAL STEPS TO GREAT CREDIT

What is the next thing to do now you have your mind open to new possibilities?

1. **List it!** List what you want in detail and write or type it out. Be specific. Your thoughts are real and living beings. Give yourself the freedom to express your deepest desires without hesitation. Be courageous. You were born that way. Claim

your power, and tranquility and peace of mind will be your constant companions.

2. **Date it!** When setting a goal, it needs to be ambitious as well as initially possible and believable so that the conscious mind's filter allows it to go through to the unconscious mind for activation. So a long term **dated** goal with a short term **dated** hook is the way to go. Always write down the exact date with the exact year too; your unconscious mind needs a time frame. "I have a million dollars in the bank on May 15th (Next Year: Two thousand and…). And to begin, I have ten thousand dollars in the bank on May 15th (This year: Two thousand and…)." Think: Long term goal, short term hook. Activation then needs to occur.

3. **Start with the tiniest step.** What is the SMALLEST possible action you can take to activate the goal? Is it one email, one phone call, or perhaps attending a breakfast meeting of people who are already successful so you can ask them for information?

4. **Model someone who is successful at it.** Research the Internet to discover people who have succeeded before you and ways that they did it, then use the information you gather in the simplest way possible. It can be done on a small budget or no budget these days. YouTube is one of the best ways to research new information fast.

FAST TRACK TO SUCCESS – D IS FOR DESIRES ACHIEVED

- Desire it, dream it, determine it and decide to do it! *Why* is this important?
- Ditto! Model someone else who has succeeded at it. EXACTLY.
- Destination. Where is this going to be accomplished? Knock it out of the park – be bold and keep it simple; clear vision, clear goals.
- Date it! Exactly…What is the exact date that it is to be completed?
- Direct it. What is the very first small step to start the process? Have confidence (pretend is your best friend!).
- Determination and Clarity. Be clear about how it is going to happen. Assume that everyone needs it. A straight no is great –leaves you time for the yes's
- Dig Deep. Have conviction that the solution is here with you now.

Done!

To increase abundance on every level you need to have an entrepreneurial mindset. That means that your focus is on making money *first*. The question to ask yourself in any undertaking is, "How quickly will I make money from this?" The financial return is optimal in three months or less. Too many entrepreneurs start with the idea of helping people first. They set up a good website, start spending money on marketing and then hope people will come, thinking that they will get fame and fortune eventually. Those things are hugely important, but more important to know is that the faster you make money, and the more you make, the more people you can help. That will bring you the recognition and rewards that will lead you to be able to help even more people, then perhaps lead you towards training others and on to philanthropy because of your amazing success.

High achievers typically have a strong belief that what they want to be, do, or have can be accomplished; they also are flexible enough to adapt when things don't always go as planned. Their vision is so great and so clear to them that small things not working as they should is almost expected if they are going to achieve their dreams. In fact, they believe that if things don't sometimes go awry then perhaps they are not aiming high enough!

It is also important to name your goal and make it feel real. Be clear about your intent and give it wings. Let it fly with a sense of strong emotion and excitement! Excitement is the hotline to God and the key to manifestation. I was living in Canada in my dream house in 2008 with my then husband and thirteen-year-old daughter. My book, *Every Word has Power*, had been successfully published. I had been working fifteen to twenty hour days, working on my PhD in clinical hypnosis in the evenings and facilitating change in people during the day, as well as looking after my beautiful young daughter while my husband worked. I had reached the end of my tether and said to him as we went to bed, "If I had just $1000 right now I'd be off to the Dominican tomorrow by myself to get my energy back." I went to bed dreaming of lying on a beach in the sunshine. I could almost taste the salt air. The doorbell rang at 9am the next morning and standing there was a lady whom I recognized. "Hello Angela." I said. "Here!" She thrust an envelope in my hand. "I took your course years ago and never paid for it! I couldn't go one more day without paying you back." In the envelope was $1000. The Dominican was wonderful!

Making friends with money is important if you are to enjoy receiving it. So how do you make positive associations with money if you have not had great experiences with it in the past?

LOVE YOUR MONEY!

Materials: Notebook, pen, clear plastic bag and $20 of change or small notes.

Put the notebook along with the pen into the plastic bag. Every time you get an AHA, or notice something wonderful, have a good time or just feel great, write briefly about the experience in your notebook and put some money in your bag. You'll start to connect money with feeling good, joy and abundance in three days! At the end of a year, or your own specific time period, go ahead and spend the money on fun, or do something wonderful for yourself.

Enjoy what you do and have passion in your life. Without passion life is a black and white still photograph. With passion and fun, life is a Technicolor surround sound movie.

The Greek philosopher Heraclitus said, "Character equals destiny." Take the initiative and design your plan to be rich and happy. You have inside you everything you need to succeed beyond your wildest dreams. YOU are the keeper of your own sacred space. YOU are the only person who can do your life well. Life requires ALL of YOU to show up every day. Expect miracles and they will come.

If you would like a private breakthrough session with Dr. Yvonne, in person or via Skype, feel free to call her or email her. Her best-selling book, *Every Word has Power*, is available on Amazon.

Contact info:
yvonne@globalwelcome.com
(416) 494-9996
www.GlobalWelcome.com.

ABOUT THE AUTHOR

Yvonne Oswald PhD, award winning, best-selling author of Every Word has Power, now in eleven languages, is at the leading edge of the new development field of Human Behavioral Technology. She is a renowned and respected International Keynote Speaker, Communications Trainer, Master Trainer of NLP, and Master Trainer of Hypnosis. U.S. National Awards include; **Most Unique Contribution to the Field of Clinical Hypnosis 2012** for her work with changing negative self-talk; and a **Visionary Award nomination for Mind Magic,** for pioneering the process of clearing a negative emotion in less than a minute.

Yvonne has an outstanding reputation for her exciting, innovative, fun, and interactive seminars for both public and private sectors.

A British born, certified teacher with 20+ years' experience, Dr. Yvonne clears challenges for every audience (live, radio, and television) and assists others to go beyond their boundaries and reach the success they desire. Her You Tube channel is available worldwide. To learn more, please visit www.GlobalWelcome.com.

CHAPTER **14**

CREDIT IS NOT WEALTH

Paul Therien

Most people look at their credit rating as simply an indicator of whether or not they pay their bills on time. While that may largely be true, it also speaks to much more about us as individuals. Having good credit is a lot like having good karma, you do good things and good things happen to you in return.

In today's world, like it or not, credit is king and the way we manage that credit has a direct impact on our ability to function as constructive citizens. You can't do much these days without credit…book a hotel room, a flight, or rent a car. Most landlords require a credit check and more and more employers are also starting to pull credit reports as a part of the recruiting process.

Credit has become much more than a simple report that tells people if we are paying our bills on time; it has become a character report.

In the 1980's, our world transformed to a highly consumeristic society where shopping has become a pasttime almost as potent as sport. We seem to have replaced the concept of living debt free in order to quench what has become an insatiable thirst to always have the newest and best of everything. We only have to look to the Black Friday riots to see a demonstration of the hold that consumerism has on people.

The term "living within one's means" has long gone out of the familiar lexicon of society. We now use credit as a way to improve our economic standing in the eyes of our peers.

Credit is more accessible today. That is a direct result of the need for consumerism. Money is spent without thought to the long term consequences of spending habits. How much debt is incurred also tells a story; one just as vivid as our payment history.

When we speak to character, it has to be known that most people who experience credit problems are good people. But when we spend our way into huge levels of debt, it demonstrates a lack of foresight and planning, or that we simply do not understand the potential negative consequences of "misusing" or "over using" credit.

Understanding credit and how it can have a dramatic impact on your life is your responsibility alone. As much as we may like to say it is the creditors, we have to be accountable for the choices that we make because ultimately we are the only ones who are responsible for the outcome of those choices.

When we make the choices that lead us down the path to debt, we choose to have the biggest and best of everything, and we choose to pay for those things using other people's money. The consequence of those choices is that we have made a promise to pay them back. They, the creditors, have a reasonable expectation that we honor that promise – no different than we would expect our friend to pay us back if we lend money to them.

If our friend didn't pay us back, we would have serious doubts about the character of our friend, and we would probably never trust them again. If anyone asked us about that person it is unlikely that we would give them a very positive reference, especially if it was about borrowing money.

Some people think that creditors are just big unfeeling corporations that don't care about the little guy. If we don't pay them back, it's not really a big deal because they are big enough to take it. The fact is that this could not be further from the truth. These credit agencies are providing a service, and yes in many cases they make a lot of money. Not paying them back however, does impact others through things like higher interest rates and higher fees. More importantly, the person most impacted is...you.

Having a low credit rating tells others that entering into a relationship with you is not safe; you don't keep your promises. You may have to give a larger deposit to obtain a service, and you certainly will not be able to finance the purchase of a big ticket item. You may even find that your future job prospects are impacted. You may not be able to rent an apartment, and you will not qualify to purchase a home. None of these are situations that are easy to deal with, and they can have a lasting impact on our self-image as well as our self-esteem. We need to be able to move forward with success to remain satisfied as individuals.

So what about negative events? Well, it is very true that these happen. We may find ourselves in situations that we have no control over; like being laid off a job. With the average person only having enough money saved to cover them for two months, income deficiency can be devastating. This is especially true if we have been borrowing our way into a lifestyle.

Less than a hundred years ago, people who did not pay their debts were considered to not belong in good society and were put behind bars in 'Debtors Prisons' and although most countries have moved past this practice, there are still several countries around the world that still have these laws in place. In fact, there are several states in the United States of America that (after their day in court and if found guilty) that still imprison people for not paying debts.

This is an extreme, and today most people who find themselves in this situation will file for bankruptcy, or work with a credit counselor as a solution. Both are great options, but will have an impact for seven years, so let me save you those seven years! There are many different options available to help you if you get into sticky situations. You can work with companies that specialize in repairing damaged credit and help to overcome the obstacles that negative ratings have on people's lives.

The key is to find a way to better manage our financial future, and that means education. Our world continues to evolve and access to money is easier today than it has ever been in history. The best solution is to be proactive, better understand credit, and plan for the unexpected events.

I believe that credit can be a powerful tool which can help propel our lives forward if we use it properly and in combination with a balanced plan. The best way for anyone to build that plan is through education and making smart financial choices.

Always remember...credit is not wealth.

You don't actually need to be wealthy today to build wealth for you and your family tomorrow. It can actually be as simple as creating a plan and sticking to it. It may take a little longer, but in the end, with your success, you will teach your children and future generations about both wealth and life management.

ABOUT THE AUTHOR

Paul started his career with Avco Financial Services over 20 years ago and since then he has gained a wealth of business experience in various industries including Vice President of Operations for Centum Financial Group and most recently as Vice President Training, Western Canada for Dominion Lending Centers. He has also acted as a senior consultant to various firms as a leadership skills trainer, and numerous other subjects.

Paul has received several honors and awards throughout his career. He is the only person to be included in the Canadian Mortgage Professionals Hot List four times from , both in 2013 to 2016. In January of 2015 he was named an Industry Icon for 24 years of service and influence in the mortgage industry and is the first national brand leader to have received this distinction.

Paul dedicates a significant amount of time to his community and has been recognized internationally for his contribution to human rights and equality and in 2011 was inducted to the Order of the Maple Leaf. He is also the Founder and Chairman of the Q Hall of Fame, Canada's national LGBT Human Rights recognition program.

CHAPTER **15**

THE ROLLER COASTER RIDE OF CREDIT

Teresa Velardi

At the age of 17, the applications started coming in. Credit card applications, that is. I was barely out of High School, or was I even out of High School?

Luckily, my parents knew the meaning and importance of developing good credit habits from an early age. Eventually, after applying for a few of the cards that were being offered, the coveted card came in the mail. Yay!!

What would I buy first? Would it be something that I needed? Something I had been wanting to get for a while and just didn't have enough money to buy right away? Would I go on a vacation? Imagine that! A vacation that I could decide to take on my own, at least where using the credit card to pay for it was concerned. Somehow, I felt as if I had this new found power in my pocketbook: a credit card.

Before I made any decisions on even making my first purchase, my parents sat me down and told me how this was a great privilege that had been bestowed upon me by virtue of the issuance of that card. "This will teach you how to manage your money and build your credit so that someday," they said, "you will be able to buy a car on your own merits, then a house, and what-ever else you may want." It seemed to me that my fi-nancial future was contingent on what I did with that magic little card.

Ultimately, I was prudent with the use of that card. I made sure that I made my payments on time, kept the balance low, and sometimes even paid it off entirely. Then came the higher credit limit and more offers, this time of pre-approved cards. WOW! Needless to say, one became two, then, two became several cards at my favorite clothing shops. Life was good, and the ward-robe was amazing!

Believe it or not, that first credit card account was open and in good standing for over 30 years. In the credit world, that's something to hang your proverbial hat on. Yes, I had bought the new car on my own merits, and been approved for the financing to build my first home. I can't say the same for the other half of the "build the new home" equation. I was able to get the loans approved because my credit score, and the way I had managed my accounts, awarded me great privilege.

And then it happened...

An unexpected event occurred, and my financial world changed. The finances were no longer there to pay for all that I had accumulated on the debt scale. It had been getting much less easy for months before I realized that I was soon going to have to be letting go of that 30 plus year credit card. I actually had an emotional attachment to that card. I know it seems illogical, but that was the start of what I considered to be a good ride on the road of life.

Now I was facing the uphill part of the roller coaster that I was about to be riding. I made minimum payments on whatever I could with what little I was able to scrape together on any and all of the cards just to keep them in play. It became a juggling act that took a lot of my energy. It seemed that the climb up the hill was taking forever. When was I going to be able to put my hands in the air and jump up and down with the excitement and joy and ease that comes on the way down that first hill? Surely there had to be some relief coming!

In a way, there was. The cards that had the most available credit began reducing the credit limits so I couldn't juggle the balances on them any longer. I know that seems a little counterproductive, yet that's what I was doing. I was juggling until I could get some money together to make this all right again. When I finally realized the stark reality, I knew I had to change. I had, after that long uphill climb, finally played out all possibilities. It was time for a new plan.

It was time to make those calls that I was definitely not looking forward to...

I figured that since I had been so mindful of the way that I used credit in the past, the credit card companies would be ready and willing to do almost anything to help me as a long term customer. After all, I WAS a customer with one of those companies for over 30 years. Even though that and a token would get me on the New

York City subway, I was able to have a conversation that would ultimately allow me to work out a plan.

With much persistence, tremendous honesty and humility about my personal situation, along with good negotiating skills, I was able to reduce the balances I owed by nearly seventy-five percent on most of the cards and more than fifty percent on others. I was also able to stop all late fees, and reduce the unbelievably high interest rates. One company even stopped ALL interest and removed some of the interest that had previously been posted to my account! Sure, my credit score took a downward turn during the process as I formed the plan to reduce my debt, but I was able to breathe again. I could finally sleep at night knowing that there was a light at the end of this credit card tunnel.

In order to follow through with what I had agreed to, I had to sell off some "stuff", borrow a little bit here and a little bit there, and promise to pay everything back. Ultimately, it all worked out. I wasn't planning on making any big purchases that would require me to use a credit card anyway. Over time, as I paid according to the plan that I negotiated, signs of my credit score being on the rise became evident. I actually began getting offers for credit cards again! I almost couldn't believe it! Although it took me a long time to even consider responding to any of them, I figured that this was a necessary step along the way towards rebuilding what had fallen so quickly.

I finally did decide to apply for another credit card after a while, and guess what? I was approved! Imagine that! I was being given another chance to rebuild that all important credit score. Yes, the interest rates were high, but it was a chance to prove my credit worthiness again. Right around that time, I had the honor and privilege of meeting my now good friend, Patricia Giankas. She introduced me to a tool that she created called "Score Navigator". It is designed to help people increase their credit scores, ultimately improving the overall quality of their lives. Through the use of this tool, and the advice the program provides, I was able to rebuild my credit score. Pretty quickly too!

Go ahead and take a look at the program. You can find it at www.scorenavigator.com. It will teach what you need to know in order to increase your score, while giving you solid advice on how much to pay and when to pay it to achieve the best and fastest results. This tool will help you wherever you are in the journey, whether you are in the credit recovery process as I am, are simply wanting to improve your score, even if you are brand new to the world of credit. You will learn how to stay in control as you take that thrill ride of credit, so you can truly experience the rush and joy and "hands in the air feeling." When you decide to take your score seriously, and make a commitment to use the information that this wonderful tool provides you, your credit and your life will improve dramatically. What a great feeling! Like me, you will be able to sleep better at night knowing that you have a fabulous, safe and secure financial future ahead.

By the way, I never did get that rush of excitement coming down the hill on that roller coaster ride I was on. In the future I'll pay for that kind of thrill at an amusement park.

ABOUT THE AUTHOR

Teresa Velardi, founder of Authentic Endeavors Publishing, is an author, editor, speaker, host of Transformational Tuesdays, coach and potter. Pottery making is a wonderful illustration for transformation; going from a ball of clay to a work of art. Using that, Teresa's coaching, speaking, writing and publishing is truly transformational.

What people share most about Teresa is her ability to connect with others. Her extensive business background, ability to focus on what's next and her unstoppable nature in the face of adversity, has brought experience and wisdom to others.

"Gratitude is the key that unlocks the door to prosperity in ALL areas of life." Teresa thanks God every day for all the blessings in her life. To learn more about Teresa and her endeavors, go to:

www.teresavelardi.com
www.transformationaltuesdays.com
www.yourstorymattersnow.com
teresa@teresavelardi.com

CHAPTER 16

DON'T JUST PAY, PAY ATTENTION!

Franklin Vanderbilt

I grew up in Chicago Illinois. My father always taught me the importance of money and the importance of saving money. When I left home, although I had this knowledge, I didn't practice it right away. There were some times when I would save and sometimes when I would spend. As a college student learning how to take care of myself, there was a bit of a learning curve to figuring things out. About a month before I left to go to Eastern Illinois University, I got my first credit card with a limit of $2500. I was excited.

It was my first time being away from home and I would be studying with professor Johnny Lee Lane, an extremely talented and highly respected percussion teacher. This would also be the first opportunity I would have to really learn how to manage money on my own.

I had to buy books and feed myself. I also had to pay for things like transportation or whatever I needed. I was amazed to see how quickly money goes if you're not paying attention. Before I knew it, I was at the limit.

I learned how powerful the use of credit could be in my late twenties when I began to pay attention and understand how to use it. I really had to watch what I was doing with my credit. At one point I tried to buy a car and got a lesson in just how important my FICO score was. I said, "All right, I really DO need to start paying attention."

When you're an independent contractor, work can sometimes be inconsistent; it's up and down. I was working as a musician, as I am now. When I realized that my credit was pretty much my ticket through life and to acquire things, I paid more attention. I would soon need an apartment, or have to buy a car and at some point in the future, I would need a home loan. Building good credit became important to me as I thought about my future. When my employment became steady, my credit got much stronger. I'm glad that I learned as a young man that great credit is one of many things we all need to get through life.

When it comes to the topic of money, one of my role models is Warren Buffett; I believe what he says. He hates credit cards. He suggests we stay away from them. Though I agree with his philosophy; I do my best to use credit conservatively. I totally understand Buffett's teaching that if you don't have the money in the bank, don't spend it. On the other hand, I have to say that my favorite credit card is American Express, because you can't keep a balance on an American Express Card. So that's why I use my AmEx card. I know I have to pay it off monthly, and I'm building my credit score with it. That's the only card I use. Yes, it's a credit card, but if I must choose one card to use, I would have to go with American Express. I am super disciplined about my spending with AmEx. The balance has to be paid in full each month and that means no interest either! Using that card has taught me how to better manage my money. I stay away from lots of credit cards because I don't want that kind of debt hanging over my head. I only like American Express.

Paying attention to my credit has taught me to spend wisely. Yes, spend wisely because you're going to have to buy a home one day and luckily when my credit score rose to the mid-700s, I got approved for home loans, twice. That was great! You must pay attention to your credit because a good score is necessary in all aspects of life. In the long run it'll work for you. Later on you'll be able to get whatever you want because your credit is strong.

Some employers check your credit history while screening as part of the job application process. Your likelihood of getting a job could actually depend on your credit score and the way you handle your money. I guess that speaks to the saying that 'how you do any-thing is how you do everything. If you can't manage your own money, how will you do when you are put in charge of someone else's money?

I've been fortunate enough to do what I love for a living and to benefit from my talent. I'm also very happy to say that because of my talent and the consistent work I've had, along with money management skills I have learned, my credit score has improved. I pay close attention to it because I realize how important a great credit score is.

When you're making money it's easy to not pay attention when the money's coming in. I think we've all been there. It's amazing how $50 here, $100 there, $200 here, $80 there adds up. If you do that each week, even each month then you start to see what you're really spending. Reality hits with a question like, "Wow I went through $5000 that fast?" It adds up. It's about daily habits and it's consistent discipline. When you develop these good spending habits then life can be easier; now and in your future.

I'm all about enjoying life and I don't believe in being cheap either; but I don't necessarily have to overspend, or make unnecessary purchases. When you can afford to do things, then by all means go ahead, have fun. Being cheap is not such a good mentality. I think everyone should find a middle ground that works for them. There is a lot to be said for being financially responsible. I can honestly say that I am glad that I "saw the light" of what it means to have great credit at such an early age.

As a professional musician, the drum set and my gifted ability to play it has allowed me to invest in myself. It is my talent and my desire to use it that has brought me to the realization that I need to be mindful of my finances and to build a great credit score over the years. I've traveled the world with lots of people. It's been an awesome experience. So pay attention and there will be awesome experiences in your future too.

ABOUT THE AUTHOR

Franklin Vanderbilt was born to drum.

Raised on Chicago's West side, Franklin's family encouraged the development of his innate musical talents.

By age five, he was seated on a Ludwig drum kit, beginning a childhood filled with music and mentoring by a host of legendary jazz and blues musicians such as Ramsey Lewis, Ernie Adams, Orbert Davis, Willie Pickens, Pat Mallenger & Clarke Terry.

After high school, Franklin attended Eastern Illinois University where he trained under renowned percussion professor, Johnny Lee Lane. Franklin began singing, songwriting and music production at the young age of twenty-four.

Franklin Vanderbilt is an accomplished drummer /percussionist who has worked with Chaka Khan, Stanley Clark, Stevie Wonder, Richie Kotzen and currently Lenny Kravitz. Franklin embraces the same passion he brings to the stage in his daily celebration of life.

To learn more about Franklin, visit his website: www.FranklinVanderbilt.com.

CHAPTER **17**

CREDIT: WHEN LESS IS MORE AND OTHER SECRETS

Barbara Yager

Would you like to know some simple facts about credit that can help you stay at the top of the credit game?

Before we begin, let me tell you a bit about me and how I am qualified to share my thoughts about credit with you. I worked in the financial services industry for over 20 years. During that span of time I worked in operations, collections/bankruptcy, lending and legal services. Through it all I learned one very important thing when it comes to the use of credit and having a great credit score. That simple truth is…"Less is More."

Everyone needs a favorable credit score to secure the best interest rates should they want to borrow money. The secret is, just because you have a great credit score does not mean you should consider borrowing all over the place. The secret is to be a selective borrower! I tell people, it is like the preverbal Catch 22. The less and more selective you borrow, the higher the score. The higher the score, the better and easier the borrowing. Crazy huh? But don't worry, let's sort this out.

The fastest way to a great credit score is having a mixture of credit accounts such as a car loan, home loan and just a few revolving credit accounts. Financial institutions love to see an active borrower. They also like to see a history of borrowing. The longer the credit lines are open, the better because it shows a strong payment history. You get credit score points for a strong payment history.

Another practice that will enhance your credit score is to pay your revolving credit balances off monthly. If you can't do that, be sure to keep the credit line below 50% of the available credit. The one thing you don't want to do is to carry high balances on your revolving credit. Credit scores may drop when you carry revolving balances greater than half your available credit line.

Having abundant available credit is key to adding points to a credit score. I have a friend who maintains a credit score well into the 800 range. His secret? He is a long time home owner who pays his revolving credit accounts off monthly. But you don't have to be a home owner to get that high credit score. A car loan will do the same. Think of longevity and consistency as important factors.

I think this is a good time to bring up several important points that are also important when it comes to maintaining a healthy credit score.

- Monitor your credit accounts by regularly pulling your credit report. There are very good consumer credit report providers including your credit bureaus who can provide this service for you. Any of them will give you a free report at least annually.
- Also you should know your credit score. Knowing your score is important if you are poised to negotiate a new credit account or are seeking to lower an interest rate. The higher the score the better the interest rate you should expect to get. Use this information to your advantage. What is an ideal score? What should we aim for? What is a not good score?
- Monitor for fraud. You don't want anyone using or taking advantage of you and your credit. A credit report will show you your credit history for at least 10 years in some cases. It will show you immediately if there is an issue.
- If you go car shopping, don't let them pull credit until you know you have a deal. Too many credit inquiries can lower a credit score. If a credit inquiry is made, a corresponding credit line needs to open for that inquiry. Otherwise your credit score may be negatively impacted.

NOW THAT I HAVE MY CREDIT REPORT WHAT SHOULD I LOOK FOR?

Getting your free credit report annually will show you your payment histories, open credit lines, closed credit lines, as well as all addresses and names associated with a particular social security number. It may also show you if your financial institution or other financial institution might have looked at your credit to consider you for various credit offers.

My advice to anyone seeking to manage a positive credit rating is to go over your credit report with a fine tooth comb at least once annually but twice a year is best. Here is a story that will demonstrate why looking at your credit is so important.

Several years ago I worked with a customer who learned that several revolving credit accounts had been opened under his name, but not by him. He started to receive calls from the credit grantors because of delinquent loan payments on several credit card accounts. That was the first time he became aware that something was not right. He had not made it a practice to check his credit report. As his primary financial institution, he came to us for help. We immediately began an investigation. Your financial institution should help and give you guidance if you discover any inconsistencies. We are your financial partners.

As part of the investigation we discovered that his son, who had the same name as our customer, except for the junior designation, was the offender. Name confusion can happen and fraud may occur especially in circumstances where family has access to credit information because they live in the same household.

It took us some time to sort all this out, and some patience on our customer's part. Eventually we were able to correct the credit issues and restore our member to his pristine credit status while reporting the negative credit to his son.

CAN YOU CLEAN UP YOUR CREDIT?

The short answer...NO! You can't "clean up" your credit. There is a distinct difference between cleaning credit and correcting errors created by fraud or error. If there is a mistake, a correction can be made. If you make a late payment you cannot "clean up"/remove what is a correct reporting. However, you can make sure it doesn't happen in the first place!

This is a good time for a bit of "behind the scenes" information concerning how "credit is corrected." Let me say loud and clear...there is NO magic way to correct deficient credit. If you made late payments, had a bankruptcy or repossession or other credit debacle you legally cannot undo, erase or correct the credit reporting. Financial institutions are legally obligated to report an accurate credit standing for all customers. Each financial institution reports monthly to its credit bureau partner the status of the credit line.

Why is it so important to report correct information? It is all about risk management. Before a financial institution loans money to anyone they want to be sure there will be a high degree of probability that they will be paid back. The risk in lending money is that it will not get paid back. That is true for a financial institution as it is for you individually.

Financial institutions cannot change a credit reporting from negative to positive unless there is a mistake in reporting. To do so does not clearly represent the credit habits of a customer. A financial institution wants a good, clear and accurate picture of how a prospective borrower will perform. That is how they manage lending risk.

A few years ago there were a host of "credit cleaning" agencies that said they could clean your credit. At first they had excellent success because they found a way to "cheat the system." How did they do it?

They found a way to bypass the credit correction system. They sent the financial institutions correction requests and often repeated requests to change the credit entry from negative to positive though the credit correction process. The credit correction process allows for a consumer, through his credit bureau, to send a request to correct an erroneous reporting. Important point...I said erroneous. Many of these corrections sought to delete negative reports. That is how the credit clearing agencies abused the system.

Once the credit correction is received, the financial institution only has a small window of time to review the request and to provide the credit bureau with their response. If the financial institution does not meet the time limit date the requested correction is made whether it is correct or not.

This underhanded manipulation of the system was used successfully for several years. As a result of the continued misuse of the system the financial institutions and the credit bureaus worked together to develop a better way to manage this process. As a result of their efforts a streamlined automated system was created that deleted repeated correction requests as well as processes to reduce time limit defaults.

While each correction request still needs to be verified by the financial institution, the paper correction process has been all but eliminated leading to a faster and more accurate consumer response.

One more important point. Correction requests originate with your credit bureau, not your financial institution. To correct an error, you have to work with the Credit Bureau who is reporting the erroneous status. There are three major credit bureaus, and depending on what part of the country you live in will dictate your primary credit bureau. The names of the three bureaus are Experian, TransUnion and Equifax.

ERRORS...

What if you find error on your credit report? If you find that an error has been made on your credit report, it is important to understand the process and requirements to make a correction to your credit report.

You will use the same correction process outlined above but you must provide proof of the mistake or error. You need to provide proof that clearly shows your payment was made on time or the credit line is not yours etc. Nothing less than verifiable proof will do. In the case of the identity confusion between the father and son, it was proof of age through birth certificate records that helped us to unwind the unfortunate truth of stolen credit identity.

Clearing up a credit error takes time, patience and good communication between your credit bureau, your financial institution and you. Go ahead and choose one person who will become your advocate in the error correction process. Collect your documents with care and keep copies of what you provide to the credit bureau and financial institution. Keep accurate records of with whom you spoke, the date and the content of the conversation. The more detailed your process, the faster the issue will resolve.

WHEN THINGS GET DARK...

I used to tell my coworkers...if you want to know what is happening in a person's life, look at their credit report. I have looked at thousands of credit reports in my career and in an instant I could tell what was happening to a person from looking at their credit report. We all hope to have good credit for all our lives, but I can tell you that just might be very unrealistic.

Credit abuse is not necessarily one of the primary factors leading to financial difficulties which result in the lowering of a credit score. There are three major life events that can trigger a dip in a credit score. Let me share them with you:

The first event involves health related issues. An unexpected incident such as a car accident can bring a lot of challenges financially. Illness in a family will also derail credit quite rapidly. We know how challenging it is to be able to afford drugs and cover health care costs in our country today. Deductibles in health care costs are still quite high. Hospital bills and subsequent collection of unpaid healthcare costs can quickly become credit score lowering events.

The second biggest challenge to a credit score comes from divorce. Many couples just stop paying on the bills because instead of two incomes supporting one home you often find that there are now two homes and not enough income to support them, the kids and still put food on the table. Unpaid bills will result in a lowered credit score as debt collection accounts are reported to the credit bureaus.

The third major challenge is an unexpected loss of income/job. Here is where the most darkness lurks when it comes to lowering a credit score because often the unused credit gets gobbled up to help support the home/family while a new job is secured. Credit scores may lower the higher the revolving balances climb. The tipping point is when you can no longer pay all the minimum balances and you begin to make late payments.

How can you maintain a stable credit rating when times get tough? Here are my top five tips.

1. Expect the unexpected. Always have some cash stashed or have valuables you can convert to cash to get you by, should you have a loss of income. I have a friend who loves jewelry. She buys what she likes, always good quality, and if needed she sells it should she need some cash. Her plan has sustained her many times and she gets the benefit of always wearing nice jewelry.

2. Have a plan "B" when it comes to making money. Have a hobby or create a service that can make you extra money when needed. One of my friends started a walking tour in her city. Each weekend she made between $200-$500, plus tips! Added benefit...she kept in great shape. She has a very healthy "secret stash."

3. Adopt the mantra "Less is More" when it comes to credit. Do everything you can to keep your revolving balances at zero or at least under one half of the designated credit limit. Pay your balances off each month if possible. Don't rely on

credit to support you for too long if you have a loss of income. It is a trap to do so.

4. Budget. I know, it's not the easiest thing to do! But you can make it fun. Get a few envelopes and label them, groceries, entertainment and rainy day/vacation. Each of these categories are the most important to budget for because they are the most likely to cause overspending if left unchecked. At the beginning of a pay period, transfer the appropriate amount of money to the envelope depending on your needs. At the end of the month, any money left in any of the envelopes can be transferred to any other envelope. Most of my friends transfer to the rainy day fund. No cheating and no borrowing from another envelope during the month! Before too long, you will see the benefit of this plan. Simple but powerful.

5. Curb back. I know, it is so challenging to think of doing without cable, or your weekly movie/dinner out. Curbing is really just eliminating what is not necessary at the time. It will not be forever. You may find that cutting back makes for a simpler life and can refocus your priorities. You can do this even when you are in the money! Let go of the things that don't have meaning to you; whether it is deleting that extra bill or getting rid of clutter.

While it seems that the topic of credit may not be a fun topic for some, I resolve to end this chapter on a positive note! While we all have concerns about what our credit scores may be, it is not the end of the world if it dives or you find yourself at bankruptcy court.

Credit is one of those things that can be revived and brought back to thriving good health. What may seem dark today can be turned to the positive in a short time with some dedicated effort. I know this to be a solid observation because I have seen this truth play out many times over in my long history working in and around credit.

I have worked with many people who went through "credit score darkness" only to find that in a year or two they had acceptable, thriving credit scores again. Credit can be restored in time, with the right attitude and careful planning.

Remember, your credit score does not define you...you define it!

ABOUT THE AUTHOR

Barbara Yager, The Happiness at Work Expert, builds company cultures filled with happy, engaged employees. Her passion is helping companies to zero in on their brand, culture, customers and employees with a heart-centered focus.

Barbara is a passionate and engaging business expert who specializes in building profitable organizational cultures. She puts her 22 plus years of business expertise to work finding the right solutions for her clients. Barbara believes that when a business has a clear picture of its Standards, Values and Attitudes, it will be very successful. Customers are drawn to businesses with heart. When you have plenty of happy customers, you will always have a robust bottom line.

Barbara offers free 30-minute consultations to prospective clients seeking a better way to do business. Contact her today for more information. Find out what adding a little heart and soul to your business can do.

Visit Barbara's websites www.criglobalcaps.com or www.findhappinessatwork.com. Your customers will thank you!.